Religion in America

ADVISORY EDITOR

Edwin S. Gaustad

OBSERVATIONS

ON THE

CHARTER and CONDUCT

OF THE

S O C I E T Y

For the Propagation of the Gofpel in Foreign Parts;

JONATHAN MATHEW, D.D.

ARNO PRESS

A NEW YORK TIMES COMPANY

New York • 1972

Reprint Edition 1972 by Arno Press Inc.

RELIGION IN AMERICA - Series II
ISBN for complete set: 0-405-04050-4
See last pages of this volume for titles.

Manufactured in the United States of America

Publisher's Note: This volume was reprinted
from the best available copy.

Library of Congress Cataloging in Publication Data

Mayhew, Jonathan, 1720-1766.
    Observations on the charter and conduct of the
Society for the Propagation of the Gospel in Foreign
Parts.

    (Religion in America, series II)
    Reprint of the 1763 ed.
    1. Society for the Propagation of the Gospel in
Foreign Parts, London. 2. Apthorp, East, 1732 or
3-1816. Considerations on the institution and
conduct of the Society for the Propagation of the
Gospel. 3. Church of England in New England.
I. Title.
BV2763.S8M3 1972   266.3   72-38456

    ISBN 0-405-04077-6

OBSERVATIONS

ON THE

CHARTER and CONDUCT

OF THE

SOCIETY

For the Propagation of the Gospel in Foreign Parts:

DESIGNED TO SHEW

Their NON-CONFORMITY to each other.

WITH

REMARKS on the MISTAKES of

EAST APTHORP, M.A. Missionary at CAMBRIDGE, in Quoting, and Reprefenting the Senfe of faid Charter, &c.

AS ALSO

Various incidental Reflections relative to the CHURCH OF ENGLAND, and the State of Religion in NORTH-AMERICA, particularly in NEW-ENGLAND.

BY

JONATHAN MAYHEW, D.D.
Paftor of the Weft-Church in BOSTON.

——Brethren unawares brought in, who came in privily to fpy out our LIBERTY which we have in Chrift Jefus, that they might bring us into BONDAGE : To whom we gave place by fubjection, no not for an hour ; that the truth of the GOSPEL might CONTINUE WITH YOU.

Ap. PAUL to the *Galatians*.

BOSTON, NEW-ENGLAND :
Printed by RICHARD and SAMUEL DRAPER, in Newbury-Street, EDES and GILL, in Queen-Street, and THOMAS and JOHN FLEET at the Heart and Crown in Cornhill.
M,DCC,LXIII.

TO

ALL the sincere Lovers of Truth, Righteousneſs and undefiled Religion, (of whatſoever Denomination amongſt Chriſtians) into whoſe Hands the following OBSERVATIONS may fall, whether in NEW-ENGLAND or elſe-where, they are, with due Reſpect and Humility, INSCRIBED by

THE AUTHOR.

The Introduction.

THERE are some men who write, and others who read controversy, merely from a wrangling disposition; without any regard to truth, right, or the importance of the matters contested. That this is a turn of mind unbecoming a Christian, and even a man, needs not be said. Others have an utter dislike to all disputes relative to the subject of religion, because they are Sceptics; thinking there is nothing of this kind worth disputing about. Only thus far they are fully persuaded, that it is a pity the world should be disturbed by such trifling debates, in the peaceable pursuit of pleasure, or of solid gain; very gravely condemning all disputants as quarrelsome people that would set the world in a flame, and making no small merit of their own indifference to all religion in general. A third sort are those good men, who sincerely love and practise religion themselves; but yet are such great lovers of peace, of such a timid make, and so apprehensive of the bad

effects

effects of contention, that they think it best
never to enter into debates on religion, or any
thing relative to it, on any occasion ; and condemn thofe who do fo, as at best imprudent,
ill-advifed perfons.

But furely, there may be just and suffici-
ent caufe for difputing, if religion itfelf is of
any great importance. We are enjoined to
contend earneftly for the faith : Nor are even
the means, modes and circumftantials of religion, wholly unworthy in all cafes to be the
fubject of controverfy. The epistles of the
apoftle PAUL, who would not have the Gen-
tiles troubled about circumcifion, or other
Jewifh rites ; and exhorted them to ftand faft
in their LIBERTY, inftead of fubmitting to
any yoke of BONDAGE, fufficiently evince
this. And if the good, peaceable gentlemen
who were mentioned above, are left to exercife their own liberty and difcretion, either to
read or not read difputes ; one would think,
they fhould allow others the like liberty and
difcretion as to writing : No one will compel
them to read, contrary to their inclination—

The author of the following pages fuppofes the fubject of them to be of real importance,
not only to the general intereft of religion in
AMERICA, but particularly in NEW-ENG-
LAND. In which refpect he is very far from
being fingular in his opinion. Indeed, none
befides thofe who think that our Forefathers
feparated from the Church of ENGLAND
without

without juſt grounds ; and that the differences ſubſiſting betwixt the people of that communion and ours, are quite immaterial, can
ſuppoſe this a needleſs controverſy.   The
proſperity, if not the very being of our NEW-
ENGLAND Churches, is eſſentially concerned
in it ; as may appear in the ſequel.

AN evident occaſion was lately given for
ſome perſon or other amongſt us to write
upon it, by a Gentleman on the other ſide of
the queſtion, who has attempted, as he tho't
proper to expreſs himſelf, " to determine it
once for all, by authentic vouchers. "   The
author of the enſuing pages pretends to no
ſuch great matters ; and would have been
ſincerely glad, if ſome perſon of greater abi-
lities and more leiſure, would have ſaved him
this trouble.   But ſome of his friends, perhaps
partial in his favor, expreſſed a deſire that he
would take ſo fair an opportunity to commu-
nicate ſome of his thoughts to the public, on
the point in queſtion.   In a word, his averſion
to controverſy has, on this occaſion, given way
to his regard to truth and juſtice, back'd in
this manner.

THO' he really believes the conſtitution,
worſhip and diſcipline of the Church of ENG-
LAND much leſs agreeable to the word of
GOD than our own ; yet he has an high veneration for many perſons of that communion,
as perſons of great learning and wiſdom, candor and piety.   He therefore requeſts that
nothing

nothing which here follows, may be confidered as a general reflection upon the people of
that perfuasion. He is also fensible that the
Society, &c. are a very respectable Body,
and to be treated with all the regard that is
confiftent with truth and juftice. But he cannot think, an implicit faith is to be placed in
any Body of uninfpired men, however great
or good ; or that there is any indecency in
examining into fome of the Conduct of the
faid Society, and comparing it with their
Charter ; that fo, if there is any real in-
confiftency betwixt them, it may appear.
This he takes to be the undoubted right of
every British fubject, as well as his own.
But tho' he propofes to lay fome of his fentiments on this fubject before the world, in
fimplicity and with freedom ; yet he declares,
it is by no means his intention to charge that
venerable Body with any *wilful, known* mif-
conduct, or improper application of monies :
And therefore he requefts the candor of his
readers, that no advantage may be taken of
any incautious expreffion that may efcape him
in the purfuit of his argument, even tho' it
fhould at firft view have the appearance of
fuch an accufation ; for it is not defigned as
fuch.

If his obfervations are futile in themfelves,
or if there is any indecency in the manner of
his propofing them, as he hopes there is not,
the difhonor will be to himfelf: And he even

wifhes

wifhes others to judge with the fame freedom
and impartiality that he intends to write.

THE reverend Mr. NOAH HOBART of *Fairfield*, in a book entitled *A fecond addrefs to the
members of the* EPISCOPAL SEPARATION IN
NEW-ENGLAND, † entered into this argument
concerning the SOCIETY's conduct ; which
he handled in a manner becoming both a truly
Chriftian Bifhop and a *Patriot* ; and deferves
the thanks of his country, as well as the high
efteem of his flock.   His book has been of fervice to me ; and wherever I make ufe of it in
the following fheets, proper acknowledgments
are made.   In fhort, Mr. HOBART wrote fo
folidly and judicioufly upon this fubject, that
it would hardly have been needful to fay any
thing farther upon it at this time, except in
conformity to that maxim, That every thing
newly publifhed on a controverted point, muft
be *anfwered* ;---unlefs it is either convincing
and fatisfactory to the *knowing*, or fo mean and
trifling, that even the *ignorant* are in no danger
of being impofed upon thereby.   Probably
there are not many, who know any thing of
the matter, that think the *former* the true character of Mr. APTHORP's *Confiderations*, &c.
And if I fuppofed they deferved the *latter*, I
fhould think my time ill employed in endeavouring to prevent their having *that effect*.
They feem to me to hold fuch a *medium* betwixt evidence to the wife, and glaring abfur-

B   dity

dity to the foolish, as to render some strictures
upon them very expedient.

THIS Gentleman's discretion is, at least in
one respect, very conspicuous ; perhaps in many.   Having taken the defence of the SOCI-
ETY upon himself in quality of an *advocate*,
the validity of his plea is then humbly submitted to his venerable CLIENTS in quality of
JUDGES. His *Considerations* are inscribed to
the SOCIETY, " in appeal to their JUDGMENT
and DECISION." And can it be supposed that
so ingenious an *advocate* as Mr. APTHORP will
lose a cause, wherein he is so happy as to have
the same honorable and venerable personages
both for CLIENTS and JUDGES ?---especially
if he has them for his WITNESSES too ; as
will appear in due time and place to be his peculiar felicity.   I should, however, have fol-
lowed him to the SAME TRIBUNAL to which
he has appealed, had I not feared it might be
thought a piece of rudeness, or kind of insult,
to inscribe to so venerable a BODY those *Observations*, the professed design of which is, to
shew that they have, in some respects, coun-
ter-acted and defeated the truly noble ends of
their INSTITUTION, however contrary to
their intention.

SECTION

SECTION I.

The QUESTION *ſtated.*

THE author of the following pages deſires to have what he diſputes about,
relative to the *charter*, SOCIETY and
their *miſſionaries*, clearly underſtood in the firſt
place. He apprehends there is no ground for
controverſy as to religious liberty, or the natural and legal right which proteſtants of all
denominations have, in any part of his Majeſ-
ty's dominions, to worſhip God in their own
way reſpectively, without moleſtation.

NOR is the queſtion, whether any perſon or
perſons in Great-Britain have a right, conſidered in their private capacity, if they think
it expedient, to encourage and propagate epiſcopacy in America, by tranſmitting money to
build churches here, to ſupport miſſions and
ſchools, or the like. Whatever our ſentiments
may be about the church of England, we are
not ſo vain as to aſſume a right of dictating to
them the manner in which they ſhall, or ſhall
not beſtow their charity ; or in any ſort to

controul

controul them herein. This is faid with reference to people in England, confidered in
their private capacity, as was intimated before.

AGAIN : The queftion is not, whether that
very refpectable Body corporate, *the Society for
the Propagation of the gofpel in foreign parts,* are
to judge for themfelves in what particular places, and under what circumftances their charity is to be employed, conformable to the true
defign of their charter. They muft, in the
nature of the thing, judge for themfelves in
this refpect, if they act with integrity, according to the nature of the truft repofed in them ;
which is not difputed. Though as this is a
matter of public concernment, in which the
civil as well as religious intereft of the King's
fubjects in America is nearly concerned ; other
people have a right to give their opinion about
the manner in which that charitable fund is
employed ; whether agreeably to the intent of
the charter or not ; and even publicly to re-
monftrate againft any mifapplications of it,
whether through mif-information, or any other
fuppofeable means, in order to a reformation
of fuch abufes, if real. Moreover ;

THERE is no difpute, but that the venerable
Society have a right to plant churches, to fupport miffions and fchools, &c. in many of the
Britifh American colonies ; or whether this is
in conformity to the intent of their charter.
No one that has ever read it, can poffibly make
a doubt of this ; or imagine that the Society's
care

care and charity ought to be confined to the heathen flaves in, or the favages bordering on the plantations.

BUT then it is fuppofed by many perfons, that there are fome of thefe American colonies, whofe religious ftate is fuch, as renders them improper objects of this charity ; and confequently, that whatever has been done by the Society in fupporting epifcopal miffions in them, is a mifapplication of that part of their fund, which has been employed in this way; to the neglect, prejudice and injury of other colonies, the Negroes and Indians, who were unqueftionably proper objects of their charity.

THIS therefore, is the main queftion now propofed for a free and candid difcuffion ; Whether the planting epifcopal churches, fupporting miffions and fchools, &c. in certain parts of America, particularly in New-England, in the manner, and under the circumftances in which this has been, and ftill is done by the Society, is conformable to the true defign of their inftitution, according to their charter ; or a deviation therefrom, and confequently a mifapplication of their fund ?

THIS is a queftion of no fmall importance : And it can be determined only by comparing the manner and circumftances in which the Society have planted churches, fupported miffions, &c. in thefe parts, with their charter itfelf. And all who are capable of underftan-

ding

ding the charter, which is very plain, and who are apprized of the facts and circumstances aforesaid, may be deemed competent judges of the merits of this cause.

That part of the charter which explains the design of the institution, will be produced in the next section. In the mean time it may be observed, that the ingenious Mr. *Apthorp* has proposed a certain question for discussion, or rather to be " determined once for all," which was probably never thought of before; and is indeed hardly intelligible. It is this, " Whether the Society—conform to the de- " sign of their incorporation, by maintaining " episcopal churches in the *settled towns and* " *villages* of North-America: or whether they " have not misapplied a fund originally *limi-* " *mited to the conversion of the heathens.*"† This he speaks of as a very interesting question to " the Missionaries and their congregations." Possibly it may be so. But what does the gentleman mean by the *settled towns and villa-ges of North-America ?* Is this designed in op-position to *unsettled,* or *uninhabited* towns and villages here ? I know of none such : But if there were any, who ever supposed that it was expected the Society should *maintain episcopal churches* in such, but not in the *inhabited* towns and villages ? It were hard indeed, to confine the pious labors of the missionaries to places without

† *Considerations on the Institution and Conduct of the Society,—&c.* p. 1.

without inhabitants !—Efpecially while there are fo many *fettled* towns and villages in North America, Indian as well as Englifh, where they might be ufeful. But by the disjunction which he makes, it feems as if by *fettled* towns, &c. he meant places inhabited by Englifh fubjects and profeffed Chriftians ; for the Society's employing their charitable fund in order to the *converfion of the heathens,* is the othe part of the disjunction ; and fo ftands in direct oppofition to *maintaining epifcopal churches in the fettled towns and villages here.* But if this is what he means by *fettled* towns, &c. the queftion feems at beft very vague and indeterminate : For fome of thefe towns and villages have all along had minifters of other proteftant communions in them ; others have not. And it was proper, one would think, that the gentleman fhould have let us know which of thefe he intended. If he meant the latter only ; and intended that the fociety rightly applied their fund in maintaining epifcopal churches in *them,* as well as in the converfion of the heathen, it is allowed ; there is no controverfy as to this. But if he meant the former alfo ; and that the Society rightly apply their fund in maintaining epifcopal churches in places where other proteftant churches were before fettled, and the adminiftration of God's word and ordinances provided for, then indeed he oppofes us. But, on any fuppofition, his disjunction is extremely lame and imperfect. And how
interefting

intereſting ſoever his queſtion may be to the *Miſſionaries and their congregations* ; yet, as he has ſtated it, the *eſtabliſhed* miniſters and churches of New-England will not probably think themſelves much concerned in it. For if the queſtion is determined only in the ſame looſe, vague manner in which it is propoſed, it can do little good nor hurt to any cauſe, even tho' it ſhould be thus determined *once for all*.

SECTION II.

Part of the Charter, *with obſervations upon it, ſhewing the true deſign of the* Society's *inſtitution.*

THE firſt thing requiſite in order to a right determination of the queſtion, Whether the Society have deviated from the deſign of their inſtitution or not, is to ſhew what that deſign was. And to this end an appeal muſt be made to their charter, granted by King WILLIAM III. in the 13th of his reign, Anno 1701. The preamble of which clearly expreſſes that deſign, if conſidered all together. The whole preamble is therefore here ſubjoined, without the omiſſion or addition of a ſingle word ; only ſuch clauſes as are eſpecially neceſſary to a right underſtanding of its deſign, are printed in a different character.

" WILLIAM

"WILLIAM the Third, by the Grace of GOD, &c.

I. "WHEREAS we are credibly informed,
" that in *many* of our plantations, colo-
" nies and factories beyond feas, belonging to
" our kingdom of England, the *provifion* for mi-
" nifters is *very mean ;* and *many others* of our
" faid plantations, colonies and factories, are
" *wholly deftitute and unprovided* of a mainte-
" nance for minifters, and *the public worfhip* of
" God; and for lack of *fupport* and *maintenance*
" for fuch, many of our loving fubjects do want
" the adminiftration of God's word and facra-
" ments, and feem to be abandoned to *atheifm*
" *and infidelity ;* and alfo for want of *learned*
" *and orthodox* minifters to inftruct our faid lov-
" ing fubjects in the principles of TRUE RELI-
" GION, divers *Romifh* priefts and jefuits are the
" more encouraged to pervert and draw over
" our faid loving fubjects to *Popifh fuperftition*
" *and idolatry.*

II. " AND whereas we think it our duty, as
" much as in us lies, to promote the glory of
" God, by the inftruction of our pleople in the
" CHRISTIAN RELIGION ; and that it will
" be highly conducive for accomplifhing *thofe*
" *ends,* that a fufficient *maintenance* be provided
" for an *orthodox* clergy to live amongft them,
" and that fuch *other* provifion be made, as may
" be neceffary *for the propagation of the*
" GOSPEL *in thofe parts.*

III. " AND whereas we have been well af-
" fured, that if we would be gracioufly pleafed
" to erect and fettle a corporation for the re-

C   " ceiving,

" ceiving, managing and diſpoſing of the chari-
" ty of our loving ſubjeċts, divers perſons would
" be induced to extend charity to the *uſes and*
" *purpoſes aforeſaid.*

IV. " Know ye therefore, that we have, for
" the *conſiderations aforeſaid*, and for the better
" and more orderly carrying on of the *ſaid cha-*
" *ritable purpoſes,*" &c.

The following obſervations are ſubmitted to
the candid reader's judgment.

1. Nothing is to be ſuppoſed the objeċt
or any part of the objeċt of this charitable and
royal inſtitution, but what plainly appears to
be really ſo, from the very words of the charter. Even tho' it were certain that thoſe perſons
to whom it was granted, had, at the very time,
ſome farther views and ends in obtaining it, beſides thoſe which are expreſſed, or plainly im-
plied; yet the words of the charter itſelf muſt
determine and limit the ſenſe of the royal *Gran-*
tor, and conſequently the legal power conferred
on the noble and reverend *Grantees*, the Society. It was *only* for thoſe purpoſes that are
particularly expreſſed, not any private or ſecret
ones, which they might poſſibly have had in
their own minds, that they were incorporated.

2. It appears that the Britiſh plantations,&c.
were really the primary, more immediate objeċt
of this inſtitution: or the King's ſubjeċts. In
which term, ſubjeċts, may be comprehend-
ed the *ſlaves* in the plantations, who are the moſt
inferior ſubjeċts. But it alſo appears that the
grand, ultimate deſign of the inſtitution was, the
propagation

propagation of the Gospel *in thofe parts;* which neceffarily includes the defign of chriftianifing the *Indians* bordering on the colonies, as a principal part of the general defign.

3. This charitable foundation was not intended for *all* the plantations, colonies and factories indifcriminately ; but for fuch of them only as really ftood in great need of relief and help in this way, and whofe religious ftate correfponded to the defcription in the charter. This diftinction betwixt the colonies, &c. is clearly fuppofed in the charter itfelf, by the manner of expreffion ufed ; particularly thofe words, " Whereas—*many* of our plantations ;" and— " *many others* of our faid plantations." Had it been faid, the *reft of them*, or *all others*, it would have materially altered the cafe. And it is at leaft probable that fome fuch expreffion would have been ufed, had it not been taken for granted, that *fome* of thefe plantations were in a quite different ftate with reference to religion.

This charity muft needs have been intentionally *limited* to thofe plantations, &c. which were or fhould be, in the ftate reprefented in the charter ; in fuch fort, that the Society had no warrant to extend it to any others, if others there were, whofe religious ftate was materially and effentially different.

4. Even amongft thofe plantations, &c. which were truly the objects of this charity, there is fome difference; for they are differently defcribed ; and come under two diftinct heads in the charter, *viz.*

Firft,

Firſt, THOSE in which the " proviſion for miniſters is *very mean:*" which are paſſed over with this curſory mention, as not being the plantations whoſe relief was principally intend-ed. [And this, by the way, naturally implies that ſome of the plantations, &c. were at that time ſupplied with *ſuch* miniſters as are deſign-ed in the charter, " learned and orthodox" ones : For there is no complaint againſt theſe miniſters *thèmſelves,* but only againſt the mean-neſs of their *ſupport.*]

Secondly, SUCH plantations as are " *wholly* deſtitute, and unprovided,*" &c. And theſe be-ing the places more eſpecially regarded in the charter, their deplorable and pitiable ſtate is en-larged upon : They are repreſented as *wholly* deſtitute of the " *public worſhip* of God ;"— " wanting the adminiſtration of God's word and ſacraments ;"—" ſeeming to be abandoned to *atheiſm* and *infidelity*"—and in danger of being perverted to " *Popiſh ſuperſtition* and *idolatry.*" Sad ſtate indeed ! but one degree better than that of pagan barbarity. And who that reads this firſt paragraph of the charter, can poſſibly doubt, but that the relief of theſe places was principally deſigned, not only in diſtinction from thoſe plantations where a tolerable pro-viſion was already made for miniſters, and the ſupport of God's public worſhip, but alſo in diſtinction from thoſe where the proviſion was " very mean ?"

5. IT is evident that, by " miniſters," or as they are afterwards called, " learned and orthodox miniſters,"

ministers," and " an orthodox clergy," were not intended ministers of any one denomination a-mongst protestants, exclusively of others. For this it may suffice at present to assign only three reasons: There will be occasion to resume the consideration of this point hereafter, when many others will be given. *First, Orthodox ministers*, in the charter, stand in direct opposition to *Romish priests and jesuits :* For it is said, that for want of the *former*, the *latter* were the more encouraged to *pervert* the King's subjects. *Secondly*, It is not said, that for want of such ministers to instruct the people in the *peculiar* doctrines, discipline and worship of the church of England, or any other particular protestant church, the Romish priests were thus encouraged; but for want of such to instruct them in the " principles of true religion" in general; or, as it is afterwards expressed, in " the christian religion." There is not the most remote hint in the charter, at any controversies subsisting amongst protestants ; but only at those which subsisted betwixt them and Roman-catholics. The evils proposed to be reme-died, or guarded against by this institution, are those of *atheism, infidelity* and *popery ;* not the errors, whether real or supposed, of any pro-testants out of the communion of the church of England. It could not even be known from the charter, that there were any dissentions a-mongst protestants ; so general, generous and ca-tholic is the language of it; and so far is it from countenancing any party-design. *Thirdly*, King
William

William himfelf was bred up in the Calviniftic principles and difcipline, quite oppofite in fome refpects to the epifcopal; and is generally fuppofed to have retained a regard for the principles of his education all along; tho' as King of England, and Head of that church, there was a neceffity of his externally conforming to its rites and difcipline. Can it be reafonably fuppofed then, that in this charter, by *orthodox* minifters, he intended thofe of the Englifh church in diftinction from thofe of all other churches in the world; and confequently to brand all the reft as *heterodox!* For this will neceffarily be the confequence; *orthodoxy* being always and only oppofed to *heterodoxy* or *herefy*. To fuppofe that *that* noble-fpirited Prince had any fuch intention, is quite unnatural: And to fay that the Grantees underftood the term orthodox in this narrow, exclufive fenfe, is to reflect upon their underftandings as well as their catholicifm.

FROM the foregoing obfervations it appears, that none of thofe plantations, &c. if any fuch there were, in which a tolerable provifion was made for minifters, tho' not of the church of England, to adminifter " God's word and facraments," and to inftruct the people in the " principles of true religion," or " the chriftian religion"—and fo, to guard them againft "atheifm and infidelity" on one hand, and " Popifh fuperftition and idolatry" on the other, were in any fort the intended objects of this charity. And therefore,

THAT if the fociety have applied any
part

part of their fund to fupport and encourage the peculiarities of epifcopacy in any fuch places, they have applied it in a manner not warranted by their charter.   And

THIS abufe is fo much the greater, if at the fame time they have either neglected to fupport God's public worfhip in thofe plantations, &c. which were exactly in the poor and deftitute condition reprefented in the charter; or to propagate the gofpel amongft the heathen bordering on the colonies.   This, if real, is a double abufe ; with-holding their charity from thofe for whom it was originally defigned, and beftowing it upon thofe whom the charter, by natural and neceffary confequence, excludes from it—The truth of thefe fuppofed facts will be confidered hereafter : In the mean time it will not be amifs to take fome notice of Mr. *Apthorp's* miftakes as to the charter, and the defign of this inftitution.

SECTION III.

Of Mr. Apthorp's *manner of quoting and reprefenting the Charter.*

THIS gentleman having intimated his intention to determine the queftion " *once for all,* by authentic vouchers ;" *(Confid.* p. 7.) fays (p.8.) " The propofed " vindication is defigned to convince the *candid.* " To confute the *obftinate,* and filence the *malicious,*

" *cious*, is not in the *power of reason.*" From a
person who sets out in this modest manner, we
have doubtless a right to expect very direct,
plain authorities, and great candor, as well as
the utmost clearness and strength of reason :
For should he fail in these respects, even those
who are neither uncandid nor malicious, may
possibly remain unconvinced. But in the next
page, just after a very heroic threatning (in
some lines from VIRGIL) what a severe and de-
served revenge he would take on some unknown
person who, it seems, had provoked him in a
news-paper ; we find him taking a method to
accomplish his grand design of vindicating the
Society, so as to convince all but the uncandid
and malicious, which does not seem the best
adapted to this end : And that is, *mis-quoting*
the charter. He there undertakes to give
the words of the charter, which, he says,
" thus *expresses* the design of their" [the Society's] " institution ;" and then goes on with
the usual sign or mark of a quotation. Nor,
indeed, do I accuse the gentleman of inserting,
as from the charter, any words that are not in it.
But whoever compares his quotation (p. 9.)
with the charter itself, or only with the preamble as it is quoted *verbatim* in the preceeding
section, will find the following particulars true :
—That he has taken the liberty to transpose
some clauses, and wholly to leave out others,
without giving the least notice of it to his reader in the usual way, by a blank or ———; and
also that he has thus omitted clauses which are
very

very material, in order to afcertain the true fenfe of the charter. For he has intirely dropped the following claufe—"and feem to be adandoned to *atheifm* and *infidelity*"—and thefe alfo—"divers Romifh priefts and jefuits are the more encouraged to pervert and draw over our loving fubjects to *popifh fuperftition* and *idolatry* ;" mifplacing the intermediate claufe concerning "learned and orthodox minifters." And yet the pointing all along in this 9th page, is as it ought to be, if the charter had been quoted *verbatim*, without any omiffions or tranfpofitions.

Now, can even the moft candid think, this gentleman dealt ingenuoufly by his readers, in thus mangling and caftrating the charter? Or can it be fuppofed that he thought the claufes thus fuppreffed, were of no ufe in afcertaining the fenfe? The importance of them is quite obvious in this refpect ; they fhew the *very fad* and *deplorable* condition of thofe places, which were in an efpecial manner the objects of this charitable inftitution ;—that they were not merely deftitute of epifcopalian minifters, but minifters of any other denomination among proteftants ; fo as to be in a manner abandoned to *atheifm* and *infidelity*, or in great danger of being perverted to *popery*. Confidered in their proper connexion, and in this view, any common man may eafily fee the importance of the claufes. But it would have ruined his defign, if it had plainly appeared from his own quotation, as it does from the charter itfelf, that the

D inftitution

inftitution was not intended for the fupport of
an epifcopal clergy, where a competent provifion
was already made for a clergy of the congregational or prefbyterian perfuafion ; but where
there was no competent provifion made for any
minifters of any denomination amongft proteftants, capable of inftructing the people in
" the principles of true religion," and fo, by
God's blefling, guarding them againft the fatal
errors of atheifm, infidelity and popery.   There
was therefore evidently an end to be ferved,
fuch as it was, by thus mangling and mutilating
the charter ; whether he had any fuch defign in
it or not.   For it would anfwer his purpofe
much beft, to have the true, and very forlorn
condition of thofe plantations, &c. kept out of
fight as much as poffible, which the royal
Founder of the Society had in his mind, and
which thofe omitted claufes fo clearly and
ftrongly exprefs ; that fo people might be the
eafier induced to believe, that any of the plantations where there was no epifcopal clergy,
were actually the objects of this charity, even
tho' they had ever fo many minifters of any
other denomination, competently fupported.
And, that this was his intention, there is hardly
any room even for the candid to doubt, when
his own words juft after this extraordinary
quotation, are confidered.   For there he deduces this as one of his " certain conclufions"
from that view of the charter which he had
given ; *viz.* " That the primary intention of
" the Society was,—to provide a maintenance
                                                    " for

" for an orthodox clergy; which (as the
" charter was obtained by the members of the
" Church of England) muft—mean a clergy of
" their own church."† It might indeed be
naturally expected that the Society, being at leaft
chiefly epifcopalians, whenever they fent miffionaries abroad, would fend thofe of their own
communion. But it will not from hence follow, that they were to fend and fupport fuch,
in any or all of the colonies indifferently,
where a competent provifion was already, or
fhould be made, for proteftant minifters of another communion. This latter is what the
defence of the fociety requires; and it is a
fophifm, perhaps undefigned, which runs thro'
the *Confiderations.* But of this more hereafter.
—If Mr. Apthorp did not perceive thofe claufes
which he has fuppreffed in fo fingular a manner, to be of any importance, I blufh for him
as a reputed Scholar: But if knowing them to
be fo, he omitted them in order to impofe upon
his unwary readers, and the better to difguife
the true defign of that excellent inftitution, I
am quite in pain for him as a Chriftian;—
efpecially as One who is by office, I would hope
by example alfo, an inftructor of others in
chriftian *fimplicity* and godly *fincerity.*

BUT whatever might be his defign therein,
which is left to his own reflections, he has not
left out enough of the charter to anfwer his purpofe. Thofe remaining claufes—" provifion for
minifters is *very mean*"—"*wholly* deftitute and
unprovided of a maintenance for minifters, and

D 2   the

† *Confid.* p. 10, 11.

the *publick worship of God*"—" miniſters to
inſtruct our loving ſubjects in the *principles of
true religion ;*—" *want* the adminiſtration of
God's word and ſacraments ;"—which are all
deſcriptive of the pitiable ſtate of the places
whoſe relief was deſigned by this charitable
foundation, are ſufficient to invalidate his
defence of the Society, without the aſſiſtance of
the clauſes ſuppreſſed in ſuch a manner. For
if it can be ſhewn that the Society maintain
many miſſions and ſchools in thoſe plantations,
&c. to which no part of this deſcription is
applicable, but quite the reverſe is true; the
gentleman muſt certainly *conſider* at leaſt *once
again*, and *reaſon* a little more cloſely, before
he will convince the candid and judicious, that
the Society have not miſapplied their fund.
The charter warrants them to maintain no miſſions or ſchools in the colonies, but in ſuch
places as anſwer to the deſcriptions in the
charter; in order to make converts to the
church of England from chriſtians of other
denominations. The charter knows of no
diſtinction amongſt chriſtians, except that of
proteſtants and papiſts: Its grand object, a truly
glorious one, is, to promote chriſtianity, conſidered in oppoſition to atheiſm, infidelity and
popery; not epiſcopacy and the liturgy of the
church of England, in oppoſition to preſbyterianiſm, &c. Tho' if the profeſſion of chriſtianity is upheld, or if the goſpel is propagated at
all, it is readily acknowledged that this muſt be
done in ſome particular way, mode or form. And
when

when epifcopalians do any thing to thefe ends, it is to be expected that they will do it in that way, mode or form, which themfelves moft approve. Neither is this the thing objected againft in the prefent argument ; but, the Society's turning their arms, as it were, againft other proteftants ; and expending a great proportion of their monies in fupporting a party.

SECTION IV.

Of fome other Things tending to explain and confirm the Senfe of the Charter, and the defign of the Inftitution aforefaid.

I. THE name itfelf by which this refpectable corporation is diftinguifhed and known, is agreeable to the fpirit of the charter as before explained: *The Society for the propagation of the* GOSPEL, &c. From this name or title any one would naturally conclude, that if heathens and barbarians were not the more immediate objects of the charitable inftitution, but only the more remote ; yet it had for its object people in very deplorable circumftances at beft : fuch as were in a manner deftitute of God's word and facraments, or the means of grace. It would never enter into any one's heart to conceive, that any part of its defign was, the building up any one proteftant church on
the

the ruins of others. Thus the name of the Society, and the charter well agree. But according to ſome things which Mr. Apthorp and others have advanced, not to ſay at preſent, according to ſome proceedings of the Society, it ought rather to have been called, *The Society for propagating the church of England, in thoſe parts where the adminiſtration of God's word and ſacraments is provided for, after the congregational and presbyterian modes.*

2. THE common ſeal of the Society, which often ſerves as a frontiſpiece to the charter, is agreeable both to the charter and name of the Society. The device is, a ſun in the upper part of a circle, ſhining gloriouſly on the world ; a natural and noble emblem of the *ſun of righteouſneſs*; of Him that ſaid, " I am the light of the world." Within the circle to the right, is a ſhip under full ſail; on the prow of which ſtands a clergyman with a book in his hand, (I ſuppoſe intended for the Bible) which he extends to a company of naked ſavages on the left, who are eagerly thronging to the ſhore, to meet and receive the bleſſing. Juſt over them is a ſcroll with theſe words, *Tranſiens adjuva nos ;* alluding to Acts xvi. 9. " Come over—and help us:" the words of the man of Macedonia, whom St. Paul ſaw in a viſion; from whence he inferred that the Lord called him " to preach the goſpel" to the heathen there. And in the outward circle or circumference of the ſeal, is the aforeſaid title or name of the Society. This is a fine device for the ſeal of ſuch a ſociety, according to its name and charter. 3. THE

3. THE fermons preached annually before the Society, in the general ftrain and tenor of them, correfpond very exactly to the noble defign of the inftitution, as before reprefented. The grand topic infifted on in them, is promoting THE GOSPEL ; the undoubted doctrines and duties of the Chriftian religion. The preachers on thefe occafions feem evidently, however, to have had the heathen in their minds, rather han profeffed Chriftians who only needed affiftance in order to the fupport of God's worfhip and ordinances: In which refpect the fermons rather coincide with the ultimate than the more immediate defign of the inftitution ; and fo harmonize rather more perhaps with the feal and name of the fociety, than with the charter. This is not faid with the leaft defign to reflect on the preachers of them, as if they had forgotten the defign of the inftitution, which is indeed kept in view in thofe fermons; tho', as was intimated before, the ultimate defign of the inftitution is much more enlarged on, than. the primary or more direct. And the grand argument infifted on, to induce good people of all denominations to affift the Society with their charity, is, the *common caufe of chriftianity ;* partly for fupporting the public worfhip of God in thofe Britifh colonies, where it could not be tolerably fupported without fuch affiftance ; but chiefly for the fake of the poor heathen flaves and favages in, or bordering on the Englifh plantations : An argument which has been handled with the greateft propriety and pathos

in

in thefe fermons; and has doubtlefs drawn
fome thoufands of pounds from proteftant
diffenters in England.

I HAVE read many of thefe excellent fermons, both the very earlieft, and thofe preached
from time to time fince; and have many of
them now by me: So that it were eafy to fill
volumes with quotations to exemplify and
prove what is here afferted concerning the
general ftrain of them. But I am not willing
needlefly to load and fwell the prefent publication, by quotations to prove what, it is taken
for granted, no perfon who knows any thing
of the matter, and either has or deferves the
leaft reputation, will prefume to deny. But by
way of fpecimen, for the fake of thofe who
may not have read any of thefe fermons, fome
extracts fhall be fubjoined from the late bifhop
BUTLER's fermon before the Society, 1739:
A great ornament of the epifcopal order, and of
the church of England; the clearnefs of whofe
head, the precifion of whofe language, and the
goodnefs of whofe heart, are fo confpicuous in
all his writings.

" No one has a right to be called a chriftian,"
fays he, " who doth not do fomewhat in his
" ftation, towards the difcharge of this truft;"
[meaning the gofpel, which he confiders as a
truft] " who doth not, for inftance, affift in
" keeping up *the profeffion of* CHRISTIANITY
" where he lives. And it is an obligation but
" little more remote, to affift in doing it in
" our factories abroad, and in the colonies to
" which we are related——   " OF

" OF thefe our colonies, the SLAVES ought
" to be confidered as inferior *members*, and
" therefore to be treated as *members* of them;
" and not merely as cattle or goods, the property
" of their mafters. Nor can the higheft pro-
" perty, poffible to be acquired in thefe fervants,
" cancel the obligation to take care of their re-
" ligious inftruction. Defpicable as they may
" appear in our eyes, they are the creatures of
" God, and of the race of mankind, for whom
" Chrift died : and it is *inexcufable* to keep
" them in ignorance of the end, for which they
" were made ; and the means, whereby they
" may become partakers of the *general re-*
" *demption*, &c.———

" THE like charity we owe to the NATIVES;
" owe to them in a much ftricter fenfe than we
" are apt to confider, were it only from neigh-
" bourhood, and our having gotten poffeffions
" in their country. For incidental circumftan-
" ces of this kind appropriate all the general
" obligations of charity to particular perfons ;
" and make fuch and fuch inftances of it, the
" duty of one man rather than another. We
" are moft ftrictly bound to confider thefe *poor*
" *unformed creatures*," &c.———

" AND it may be fome encouragement to
" chearful perfeverance *in thefe endeavours*, to
" obferve, not only that they are our duty, but
" alfo that they feem the means of carrying on
" a great fcheme of providence, which fhall cer-
" tainly be accomplifhed. For *the everlafting*
" GOSPEL *fhall be preached to every nation :*

E " And

" And *the kingdoms of this world fhall become*
" *the kingdoms of our Lord, and of his Chrift.*"

AFTER difcourfing for two or three pages,
concerning the good effects that might be reafonably expected from thefe pious endeavours to
propagate chriftianity, he goes on thus—" The
" defign before us being then unqueftionably
" good, it were much to be wifhed that ferious
" men *of all denominations would join in it.* And
" let me add, that the foregoing view of things
" affords diftinct reafons why they fhould. For,
" firft, by fo doing, they affift in a work of the
" *moft ufeful importance,* that of fpreading over
" the world the SCRIPTURE ITSELF, as a
" DIVINE REVELATION: and it cannot be
" fpread under this character, for a continuance,
" in any country, unlefs CHRISTIAN CHUR-
" CHES be fupported there; but will always,
" more or lefs, fo long as *fuch* churches fubfift;
" and therefore their fubfiftence ought to be
" provided for. In the next place, they [*viz.*
" ferious men *of all denominations*] fhould re-
" member, that if CHRISTIANITY is to be
" propagated at all, which they acknowledge it
" fhould, it muft be in *fome particular form of*
" *profeffion.* And tho' they think *ours* liable to
" objections, &c.—Upon the whole therefore,
" *thefe perfons* would do well to confider, how
" far they can with reafon *fatisfy themfelves* in
" neglecting what is *certainly right,* on account
" of what is *doubtful,* whether it be wrong"—†

THUS

---

† Edit. p. 14---22. See alfo p. 24, 25,

THUS Dr. BUTLER, with his ufual penetration and accuracy, reprefents the true defign of
this noble inftitution, in its whole view, com-
pafs and extent. And how cogent is his reafoning, to induce ferious men *of all denomina-*
tions in England to join in, and contribute towards carrying it into execution, upon the true
original plan? But let me juft afk by the way,
what force there would be in this excellent reafoning, to induce proteftant *diffenters* in England to affift the Society, upon fuppofition it
was a known fact, that the Society deviated very
effentially from this noble plan, by applying a
large proportion of their fund in fupporting a
party in America, and undermining the congregational and prefbyterian churches here?
Could it be reafonably fuppofed, that thofe of
the fame religious principles in England, would
affift the Society in any defigns or endeavours
againft their brethren in New-England? or in
promoting epifcopacy here, in oppofition to the
churches of their own denomination? Or could
any preacher on thofe occafions, who knew this
to be fact, with integrity and uprightnefs make
ufe of arguments of this catholic ftrain, in order
to get money out of the pockets of Englifh diffenters? I am fully perfuaded that the great and
good Bifhop BUTLER would have detefted fuch
an artifice, and even the whole fcheme of planting and fupporting epifcopal churches in divers
places in America, had he been apprifed of the
true ftate of religion in them.—The foregoing
extracts from his fermon, as was intimated be-

fore,

fore, are given only as a fpecimen of what is
the ufual ftrain of the fermons preached on the
fame occafion.   Tho' I am not infenfible, that
fome of them, efpecially within the laft twenty
years, have expreffions in them of a much lefs
catholic ftrain, and quite aliene from the fpirit
of the charter ; an example or two of which
may perhaps be given hereafter.   But then, it
is to be obferved, on the other hand,

4. THAT in fome of thefe anniverfary fermons, all narrow, party defigns are condemned
and difclaimed in very ftrong terms ; and a zeal
for catholic chriftianity recommended in oppofition to every thing of this kind.   Thus particularly Dr. BEVERIDGE, Bifhop of St. Afaph,
in his fermon before the Society, 1706, after
commending the zeal of the primitive Chriftians,
fays, " But then we muft take care, that our
" zeal be as theirs was, according to knowledge
" —Not for any *private opinion, party* or *fac-*
" *tion*, not for either fide of a *doubtful difputa-*
" *tion*, or for unwritten traditions, wherein men
" are *apt to fpend all their zeal*, fo as to have
" little or none left for that which is the *proper*
" *object of it*.   But as it is faid of *Phineas*, in
" his great commendation, that he was zealous
" FOR HIS GOD, Num. xxv. 13. So muft WE
" be."† Another Bifhop of St. Afaph, as quoted by Mr. HOBART, ‡ (which of them I am
not certain) expreffes his indignation againft the
church of Rome, on account of the party defigns and views with which they fend miffionaries
about the world, in the following terms.
" THEIR

† 1 Edit. p. 8.   ‡ *Second Addrefs*, p. 131.

" THEIR miffions do not feem to be managed
" with an *apoftolical fimplicity*. THEY fettle
" themfelves in nations which are *Chriftians al-*
" *ready*, and have been fo from the *beginning*.
" And, under the *pretence* of converting the in-
" fidels that are among them, their *chief bufi-*
" *nefs* feems to be to apply themfelves with all
" their arts to pervert the Chriftians themfelves
" from their *ancient faith* ; and to draw them
" over to a fubjection to the *Pope* : The want
" of which fubjection is what they think the
" greateft error they find among them, and
" which they zealoufly endeavour to eradicate,
" while the Infidels are *very fparingly*, (if ever)
" *applied to by them.*" Mr. HOBART makes a
a pertinent remark to the prefent purpofe, on
Dr. WADDINGTON's fermon before the Society, which the author has not by him.   " Dr.
" WADDINGTON," fays he,—" fuppofes that
" fome would object, that *not chriftianity itfelf,*
" *but the faith and practice of* ONE COMMUNI-
" TY ONLY *of Chriftians, would be propagated*,
" and in replying to it he fays, *no fuch* PARTI-
" CULAR DESIGN *is mentioned in our charter.*"‡

   Now it is to be obferved, that thefe anniverfary fermons are almoft always preached by
members, and printed and difperfed by order of
the Society : A principal defign of them being,
to fhew what a noble and generous work they
are engaged in ; that fo people of all denominations amongft proteftants may be encouraged to
bear a part with them in it, by their donations,
legacies &c.   How great therefore muft be the
                                        furprize

‡ *Second Addrefs*, p. 143.

ſurprize of good people on the other ſide of the
water, if they ſhould find, that notwithſtanding theſe generous profeſſions of the Society
from time to time, and their diſclaiming all narrow, party deſigns, they had actually been many years proſecuting ſuch a deſign themſelves in
America ; a ſcheme not ſufficiently unlike to
that which they condemn ſo juſtly in another
famous ſociety, that *De propagandâ Fide* ; and
that they had employed a great part of their collections, revenues, &c. in carrying it into execution! That what is here mentioned only by way
of ſuppoſition, is not ſo remote from certain
fact, as many may think it even from the loweſt
probability, will be ſhewn in the following ſections—[The Society have, however, all along
profeſſed a particular regard for the church of
England ; ſuch an one as all perſons who are
ſincere, muſt be ſuppoſed to have for their own
communion : And nothing which has been ſaid
before, is to be undeſtood as a denial of this.]

SECTION V.

Some general Account of the State of Reli-
gion in New-England, before and ſince
the incorporation of the Society.

HAVING in the preceeding ſections taken
a view of the charter, and repreſented it
in its true light, in oppoſition to Mr. *Apthorp's*
miſquotation

mifquotation and mifreprefentation of it; and
alfo confirmed that fenfe which has been given
as the true, by the name and common feal of
the Society, as alfo by the anniverfary fermons
preached before, and difperfed by them, to get
fubfcriptions, &c. It will now be proper to
come to fome facts relative to the conduct of
the Society in planting churches, and fupporting miffions in America.   And as the principal
objection lies againft their conduct as to New-
England, it will be neceffary, in order to fet the
objection in a fair and true light, in the firft
place to make fome remarks on the ftate of religion here, before the Society fent any miffionaries into thefe parts, and fince.   This is
propofed in the prefent fection.   And,

 1. IT is well known, that the firft fettlers of
New-England were fuch as came hither chiefly
on account of their fufferings for non-conformity to the church of England.   They fled hither
as to an affylum from epifcopal perfecution, fe-
conded by royal power ; which often conde-
fcended to be fubfervient to the views of domi-
neering prelates, before the glorious revolution.
That this was the occafion of their flight hither,
appears even from the Society's own publications.   Thus in the *Account of the foundation,
proceedings and fuccefs of the Society,* publifhed
Anno 1706, it is faid, (p. 10.) " *It muft be ac-*
" *knowledged,* that it was the unhappinefs of New
" England and the adjoining parts, to be firft
" planted and inhabited by perfons who were
" generally difaffected to the church by law
                                    " eftablifht

" eſtabliſht in England ; and had *many of them*
" taken *refuge* or *retirement* in thoſe parts, on
".account of their *ſuffering* for non-conformity
" here at home." This faƈt muſt indeed be *confeſſed*; and that it was their *unhappineſs* to ſuffer
thus, ought to be confeſſed alſo. But, that it was
the unhappineſs of New-England to be firſt planted and inhabited by theſe conſcientious non-con-
formiſts to the eſtabliſhed church of England, is
not ſo clear a point : Neither is it to be wondered at, if they were *diſaffeƈted* to ſuch a cruel,
perſecuting church as that was before the revolution.

2. It is no leſs certain that theſe *refugees*
were very far from being perſons of a looſe, irreligious charaƈter. Had they been void of conſcience toward God, they would not have ſuffered ſo much for non-conformity, and fled
their dear native country, for the ſake of ſerving him without fear in a wilderneſs. If they
had been perſons void of religious principle, they
would in all probability have lived and died in
the communion of that church, for diſſenting
from which they ſuffered ſo much.——That they
were a ſober, virtuous and religious ſet of people
in general, is certain : Tho', that they were per-
feƈt, or free from all human errors and frailties,
is not pretended.

3. It is well known that they very early
made proviſion for the public worſhip of God,
and founded a ſeminary of learning, which has
been encreaſing and flouriſhing to the preſent
time. The zeal which they ſhewed both for
learning

learning and religion, from the firft, was indeed very uncommon ; and greatly to their
honor.   The public worfhip of God, and the
adminiftration of his word and facraments,
have all along been provided for in New-
England : I mean, in the Province of *Maffa-*
chufetts-Bay and in *Connecticut* ; which two
may contain perhaps about eight parts in ten
of the inhabitants of New-England.   In the
other two fmall governments, *New-Hampfhire*,
and *Rhode-Ifland and ProvidencePlantations*,there
has, to be fure, been much lefs care taken for
the fupport of a public worfhip.   But in the
Maffachufetts and *Connecticut* the public profeffion of religion has all along been very regularly upheld,   nearly after the fame mode of
profeffion.   The doctrines almoft univerfally
profeffed in both, are and ever have been, very agreeable to the doctrinal articles of the
church of England.   Their external polity,
and form of worfhip, are indeed known to be
different ; the churches of the *Maffachufetts-*
Bay, the principal New-England government,
being generally of the *congregational* perfwa-
fion, which the epifcopalians affect to reproach
under the name of *independency* ; and thofe in
Connecticut, of the *presbyterian* ; or at leaft ap-
proaching nearer to the eftablifhed church of
Scotland.

   4.   IT is farther to be obferved, that in thefe
two principal governments of New-England
there has been, not only provifion, but *legal*
                         F   provifion

proviſion made for the ſupport of a *learned* and *orthodox* miniſtry, and of ſchools; and that, before the Society for propagating the goſpel had a being. Particularly in the Maſſachuſetts, there was a law enacted in the 4th of WILLIAM and MARY, for thoſe purpoſes; which having been nine years before the Society obtain'd their charter, it will be needleſs to look any farther back for a *civil* eſtabliſhment of religion here, upon this occaſion. Some extracts from the law aforeſaid may be ſeen in the margin †.

5. DIVERS

† The act is intitled, *An act for the* SETTLEMENT *and* SUP-PORT *of* MINISTERS *and* SCHOOLMASTERS. It begins thus, " Be it ordained by the governor, council, and re-" preſentatives convened in general court or aſſembly, and " by the authority of the ſame, That the inhabitants of each " town within this province ſhall take due care from time " to time, to be provided of an ABLE, LEARNED, OR-" THODOX miniſter or miniſters, of good converſation, to " diſpenſe the word of God : which miniſters ſhall be SUI-" TABLY encouraged, and SUFFICIENTLY ſupported and " maintained by the inhabitants of ſuch towns "——It is provided in the ſame paragraph, that all *contracts* which had been or ſhould be made by towns, relative to their miniſters or ſchoolmaſters, and their maintenance, ſhould be " made ". good, &c. And where there is no contract reſpecting the " ſupport and maintenance of the miniſtry, or when the " ſame happens to be expired, and the inhabitants of ſuch " towns ſhall neglect to make ſuitable proviſion therein," then the court of quarter Seſſions is impowered and directed " to order a competent allowance to ſuch miniſter ;" and the manner in which the aſſeſſment ſhall be made, &c. is pointed out.

In the next paragraph it is ordained, that if any town ſhall be deſtitute of a miniſter " qualified as aforeſaid,"—" ſix months"—the ſaid court of quarter-ſeſſions, after ta-king

5. Divers acts, relating to the settlement and support of the gospel ministry here, having received the royal sanction, our churches seem to have a proper *legal* establishment. And it ought to be particularly remembered, that the act aforesaid was passed about nine years before the Society's charter was granted. Can it then be supposed that this province, where such provision was made for the settlement, support and maintenance of an " able, learned, orthodox ministry," was either one of those plantations intended in the Society's charter, where the provision for ministers was " very mean ;" or one of those which were " *wholly* destitute and unprovided of a maintenance for ministers ;" so that the King's subjects " seemed to be abandoned to *atheism* and *infidelity ;*" or were, for want of *learned* and *orthodox* ministers to instruct them " in the principles of true religion," in imminent danger of being perverted to " popish superstition and idolatry ! Certainly the charter cannot in reason be suppo-

F 2   sed

---

king certain steps to induce the inhabitants to conform to the law in respect of the settlement of a minister, shall, if this proves ineffectual, themselves " take effectual care to " procure and settle a minister qualified as aforesaid, and " order the charge thereof, and of such ministers MAINTE-" NANCE to be levied on the inhabitants of such town."

It is afterwards enacted, that every town having " fifty " housholders or upwards, shall be constantly provided of a " *Schoolmaster* to teach children to read and write." But towns that have " one hundred families," are obliged to be provided with " Grammar-schools." &c. And suitable penalties are ordained in case of neglect.

fed to have had the leaft reference to this province, or any other Britifh plantation, where a fimilar provifion was or fhould be made for the adminiftration of God's word and ordinances.

6. CHURCHES and fchools have from time to time been founded, and are continually multiplying in New-England, in conformity both to the pious inclinations of the inhabitants, and to the legal provifion made for thofe purpofes. A competent number of young men have alfo been educated from time to time in the Colleges of Maffachufetts-Bay and Connecticut, for the fupply of both. And our *ordinations* are carried on in a regular, orderly and *fcriptural* way ; at leaft according to our own conceptions : And we have doubtlefs as good a right to judge for ourfelves as to that matter, as the Society have to judge for us.

7. THE people of New-England, particularly in thofe two principal governments of it, are all in general profeffed Chriftians. There is no fuch monfter as an *Atheift* known amongft us ; hardly any fuch perfon as a *Deift*. And as to the fuperftitions and idolatries of the church of *Rome*, there neither is, nor has been the leaft danger of their gaining ground in New-England. The Congregationalifts and Prefbyterians are known to hold them *at leaft* in as great abhorrence as the Epifcopalians do. And fince the revolution, hardly a Roman-catholic, except fome few tranfient perfons, has been

been feen in New-England, till after remo-
ving the French from Nova-Scotia, and dif-
perfing them in the colonies. Thefe are a
plain, fimple, ignorant people, who have now
no Romifh priefts or Jefuits amongft them ;
and by whom we are furely in no danger of
being perverted from the proteftant faith.
How much better then, in all thefe refpects, is
the ftate of religion amongft us, than it is even
in England, under the immediate eye and documents of the venerable bifhops ? where,
notwithftanding all their pious endeavours,
there are fo many Roman-catholics,Infidels and
Sceptics, if not right down Atheifts ! It may
be added, that the common people in New-
England, by means of our fchools, and the
inftructions of our " able, learned, orthodox
minifters," are, and have all along been, phi-
lofophers and divines in comparifon of the
common people in England, of the communion of the church there eftablifhed.   This is
commonly faid by thofe who have had an opportunity perfonally to inform themfelves :
And a rationale might be given of the fact, e-
ven without any reflexion on the church
aforefaid.

8. As to practical religion, tho' we have
no caufe for boafting, yet, to fay the leaft,
we have no caufe for blufhing on a comparifon
of our morals with thofe of the people in
England, in the communion of that church :
And many vices that are common there, are
almoft

almoft, if not quite unknown here. So that if we appeal to fact and experience, there is much lefs danger of irreligion in principle or practice, and of Romifh fuperftition and idolatry prevailing in New-England, amongft the Presbyterians and Congregationalifts, for want of learned, orthodox and pious minifters " to inftruct them in the principles of *true religion,* " than there is of their prevailing in England: Tho' in the *Abftracts* annexed to the bifhop of Clogher's fermon before the Society, 1714, (p. 53.) there is indeed an intimation that the *Epifcopalians* in America are in imminent danger of falling into thofe errors, for want of bifhops to refide amongft them. And fhould any be fent hither, to prevent thefe evils amongft the people of that communion, it is to be hoped they will have better fuccefs in fo pious an undertaking, than the bifhops have hitherto had in England—

9. From the foregoing faithful, tho' brief reprefentation of religion in New-England, from the time that the firft fettlers of it were perfecuted out of England by the eftablifhed church, to the prefent, (I fpeak particularly of the two principal governments of New-England) it appears that there neither is nor has been any occafion for the Society to fupport miffions and fchools here ; and that they had not even a warrant for doing fo, by their charter. New-England (the two fmall governments of New-Hampfhire and Rhode-
Ifland

Ifland excepted) does by no means anfwer to the defcription of thofe plantations, &c. in the charter, for fupporting " God's public wor-fhip " in which, a charitable provifion is there-by made.

If it fhould be faid, (which is the moft plaufible thing that can be faid) that in fome parts even of the Maffachufetts and Connecti-cut, the provifion made for the maintenance of minifters has been " very mean, " and that therefore they come within the true defign of the charter; feveral things may be obferved in anfwer hereto. Firft, good minifters of JESUS CHRIST, who have the intereft of religion at heart, do not afpire after worldly *riches*, *pomp* and *grandeur*. Secondly, the provifion for minifters here, tho' not to be compared with the rich benefices in England, has not yet been fo " very mean," but that a competent number of learned and orthodox minifters have been found to fupply our churches. Thirdly, the government here, which took the fupport of minifters into confideration be-fore the Society was founded, muft in reafon be fuppofed more capable of judging, what a competent provifion for them is, in this coun-try, than the venerable Society. But, fourth-ly, if notwithftanding this legal provifion, a number of them in fome of our poor, fmall, or frontier towns, have been " very meanly " provided for; (which is not denied) and this is alledged as bringing fuch places within the true

intent

intent of the charter; I will allow the pertinence and validity of the argument, upon either of the two following fuppofitions. Firft, that the charitable Society have remitted fomething from time to time to *our* poor, tho' learned, orthodox and pious minifters, fettled in *fuch* places, for their help and encouragement; which would have been quite agreeable to the fpirit of the charter, and the catholic principles of the royal *Grantor*, however aliene it might poffibly have been from the principles and views of the epifcopal *Grantees*. Or fecondly, if it appears that the Society have actually eftablifhed their *own* miffions in fuch poor, little or expofed places only, inftead of doing it in our richeft and moft populous towns, where the beft provifion was before made for minifters. But if neither of thefe things can be made to appear, it will be in vain, and indeed a piece of hypocrify, to allege the " very mean " fupport of minifters here, as an argument for the Society's applying a great part of their revenue for the maintenance of God's public worfhip in New-England.

That there was very little, or rather no occafion for Miffionaries in New-England, Mr. HOBART has very pertinently produced the teftimony of the pious and judicious Dr. BRAY, who, before the Society's incorporation, was the bifhop of London's commiffary in Maryland. This worthy divine took great pains to inform himfelf of the ftate of religion in
the

the colonies, and their various exigencies ; of
which he publifhed an Account, and delivered
it as the refult of his inquiries, that " from
" New-York northward, he found *very little*
" *need* of miffionaries for the propagation of
" chriftianity ; and in the colonies of Connec-
" ticut and the Maffachufetts NONE AT ALL"†.

THIS teftimony of Dr. BRAY ought to have
the more weight, not only becaufe he was fuch a
leading man with reference to the charitable inftitution aforefaid, as to have been honoured
with name of " the Father of the Society"; but
becaufe of the great refpect with which I find
the Society fpeaking of him, of his conduct in,
and his account of the Affairs of America, in
the following words— " The Lord bifhop of
" London—did afterwards fend over the Rev.
" Dr. THOMAS BRAY, as his commiffary to
" Maryland ; who being affifted—did fettle and
" fupport feveral new minifters in that province,
" and did fix and furnifh fome parochial libra-
" ries, and did other public fervices, of which
" he has himfelf given a TRUE and modeft
" account ‡".

IT is fubmitted to the judgment of the impartial reader, whether the aforefaid teftimony
of Dr. BRAY, fo inquifitive, obferving and active
a man, is not more than a balance to the teftimony which Mr. *Apthorp* produces from the
Dean, afterward bp. BERKLEY's fermon before

G   the

† Vid. *Second Addrefs*, &c. p 126.
‡ *Account of the Society*, p. 14.

the Society ;—" that the likelieft Step towards converting the heathen, would be to begin with the Englifh. The miffionaries do good fervice in bringing them to *a ferious fenfe of religion,*" &c †. The excellent Dr. BERKLEY lived a re-clufe, ftudious life the greateft part of the time he was in N. England ; and that in the fmall govern-ment of Rhode-Ifland, where there was indeed then but little of the *face* of religion,—except perhaps among our good *friends* the *Quakers*— Befides ; he does not fpeak particularly of N. England,or any part thereof, but of the colonies in general ; thinking that the miffionaries in them do good fervice in bringing the Englifh to a *ferious fenfe of religion.* Which is doubtlefs true as to fome of the colonies : Tho' the peo-ple of the Maffachufetts and Connecticut had at leaft as *ferious a fenfe of religion,* long before there was a fingle miffionary in them, as they have had fince. And Dr. BRAY is exprefs, that in thefe two colonies, there was no occafion AT ALL for miffionaries *to propagate chriftianity :* And the Society fay, he gave a TRUE account of things in America. So that if they fend miffionaries into thefe colonies, it cannot be fo much to propagate *chriftianity,* as to propagate *fomething diftinct from it, viz.* the *peculiarities* of the church of England.

† *Confiderations,* p: 19.

※※※※ ※※※※※※※※※※※※※※※※※※

SECTION

SECTION VI.

Observations on the Conduct of the Society in supporting Episcopal Missions and Schools in New-England, *particularly in the* Massachusetts-Bay *and* Connecticut.

THAT the Society have *chiefly* sent their missionaries into those British plantations where they were much needed, according to the true design of their institution ; and that they have hereby served the interest of religion in them, is by no means denied : It were very criminal to deny them the praise that is justly due to them in this respect. But, that they have deviated from their original plan according to the charter, in some other respects ; and thereby left undone much of the good which they might probably have effected, with the ordinary blessing of God, may perhaps be equally evident from this and the following sections. Most of the following facts are very notorious, even from the anniversary sermons, *abstracts,* and other publications of the Society ; so that they will not be denied.

1. For several years, I think about eight or nine, after the Society was founded, they sent no missionary into N. England. Which may naturally be looked on as one argument, that it was not originally considered among those plantations which

　　　　which

which were fuppofed to ftand in need of their charity †.

2. THEY have from time to time, fince they began to fend miffionaries into thefe parts, been adding to their number, fupporting epifcopal fchools, &c.

IT is alfo to be obferved, that a very *large proportion* of their miffionaries have fallen to the fhare of N. England ; in the two principal governments of which, Dr. BRAY, the Father of the Society, thought there was no occafion for *any at all.* The gradual increafe of the miffionaries, catechifts, &c. in N. England, appears from the *abftracts* to have been as follows, *viz.*

	In	1718	- - -	3.
		1727	- - -	10.
		1730	- - -	14.
		1739	- - -	22.
		1745	- - -	24.
		1761	about	30.

I have feen no later *abftract.*   How

† There was no church of E. in N. E. till about the year 1678 or 1679. in the reign of the unhappy, infatuated Roman-catholic K. *James* II and the adminiftration of the Roman-catholic Governor Sir *Edmond Andros,* in this Province. It was at this time that " the Ld. bp. of London, upon an addrefs of feveral " of the inhabitants of *Bofton* did prevail with his Majefty " [aforefaid] that a church fhould be allowed in that town, for " the exercife of re'igion according to the church of E." [*Account of the Society,* p. 11.] If I miftake not, there was no miffionary from the Society in N. E. till about the year 1710 It is not material : In the year 1718 there were only three of them in all N. E. *viz.* one at Rhode Ifland another at Marblehead, and a third at Newbury ; according to the *abftract* for that year, p. 44.

How *large* a proportion of missionaries, &c. this is for N. England, compared with the other colonies, especially when a due regard is had to their religious state respectively, may appear by the single cast of the eye on the table following. In the last mentioned year, 1761, according to the *abstract*, their numbers in the southern colonies; where they were so much needed, were,

In	New-York	16.
	New-Jersey	10.
	Pennsylvania	9.
	N. Carolina	5.
	S. Carolina	5.
	Georgia	1.
	Bahama Islands	1.
	Barbados	2.

It does not appear from the *abstracts*, that the Society have any missionaries at all in the other W. India Islands, where, as is commonly reported, there is hardly any shew of public worship kept up, of any kind ; and where there are so many thousands of Negro slaves in total ignorance of christianity. The true cause of this neglect may be seen hereafter.

3. It is notorious that the missionaries, instead of being sent to the frontier and other poor Towns in N. England, where the provision and accommodations for ministers were the *meanest*, have generally been station'd in the oldest, most populous and richest towns, where the *best* provision was before made for ministers ; where the

the public worſhip of God was conſtantly and regularly upheld, and his word and ſacraments duly adminiſtred according to the congregatio-nal and preſbyterian modes. This will be evi-dent to all that are in any meaſure acquainted with this country, from the bare mention of ſome of the places where the Society ſupport miſſions and ſchools ; *viz.* Boſton, Cambridge, Salem, Marblehead, Newbury, Portſmouth in New-Hampſhire, Braintree, Scituate, Briſtow, Portſmouth in Rhode-Iſland, N. London, Strat-ford, Fairfield, Middletown, &c. I have alſo underſtood that there is a church of England in N. Haven, the ſeat of the College in Connec-ticut ; tho' I do not find by the *abſtracts*, that there is yet any miſſionary fixed there. It is not denied, however, that there are a few miſſions eſtabliſhed in N. England, particularly in Rhode-Iſland government, where they might be needed.

4. It needs not to be proved, but only re-membered, that theſe miſſions, &c. have not been ſupported, but at a large annual expence of the Society. The amount of the ſalaries here, excluſive of books to be diſtributed, &c. for the year 1761, was about £. 1270 ſterling, according to the *abſtract*. The other expences of the Society for N. England being added hereto, might probably make up the ſum of £.1500 ſterl. *communibus annis*, for many years paſt : Tho' I pretend not to be very exact in this calculation.

5. To

5. To thofe who are well acquainted with N. England, and the manner and circumftances in which epifcopal churches have been gathered and founded here, it appears that the Society have manifefted a *fufficient* forwardnefs to encourage and increafe *fmall difaffected* parties in our towns, upon an application to them ;—in thofe towns, I mean, where a regular, legal and due provifion was already made for the fupport of God's public worfhip. Some of thefe little parties, or rather factions, it is well known here, have taken their rife from no fixed principle of a confcientious diffent from our manner of worfhip, but from mere levity, petulance or avarice ;—from fome trifling, groundlefs difguft at the ftated minifter ; or a diffatisfaction about pews and rates ; or at their being under, or likely to come under cenfure for their immoral practices. I do not affirm pofitively, that either of thefe has always been the cafe, without exception : But, that it often has been, is as well known amongft us, as a thing of that nature can be known. Thefe people being thus affronted and angry without caufe, prefently declare for the *church,* without really knowing any thing of the ftate of the controverfy ; and apply to fome miffionary or miffionaries, to recommend them to the charity of the Society. And divers of the miffionaries have been much injured, (which there is no reafon to fuppofe) if they have not been very bufy in intrigues in order to foment thefe divifions and parties, *for the good of the church* ; yea,

been

been at the bottom of them. In which they perhaps thought, they conformed to the true defign of that ftanding direction of the Society to their miffionaries ; *viz.* " That they fre-" quently vifit—thofe that *oppofe* them, or *dif-*" *fent* from them, to convince and reclaim " them—" They add indeed, " with a fpirit of " meeknefs and gentlenefs"; which feems not to have been fo much remembered in all cafes, as the other branch of the direction.

But from whatever caufe thefe little difcontented parties have generally taken their origin, in towns where there were learned and orthodox minifters duly fupported ; thus much is certain, that they have not only been recommended to the Society from time to time, but been encouraged thereby, and had miffionaries fent to them. The number of thefe humble fupplicants in a town, have fometimes not exceeded eight, ten or twelve heads of families ; and this in towns confifting of two or three hundred families. It is commonly, and I believe truly faid, that there are fcarce fo many as ten families in the town of Cambridge, which ufually attend the fervice of the church lately fet up therein, but about half a quarter of a mile from the College, and from the meeting-houfe there. What is this but fetting up altar againft altar ? And fome there are, who think the principal end, and true fpirit of that miffion was not ill explained by an epifcopalian, who, as is reported, expreffed himfelf thus on the occafion— " I

don't

" don't care for them ; we have now got a church
" in the very *munns* † of 'em." It is a known
fact, that in some other churches, which, according to the *abstracts*, have been represented as
growing, flourishing, and increasing in reputation
for near half a century, the number of stated
worshippers at this day very little, if any thing,
exceeds ten or twelve families. These small
parties thus encouraged and supported by the
Society in different parts of New-England at a
great expence, have in short all the appearance
of entering wedges ; or rather of little lodg-
ments made in carrying on the crusade, or spiri-
tual siege of our churches, with the hope that they
will one day submit to an episcopal sovereign.
And it will appear at least probable in the sequel,
that this has long been the formal design of the
Society ; and that it is the true plan, and grand
mystery of their operations in New-England.

6. IT is well known to us in New-England,
that after supporting and encouraging these little parties, till in some places they have, by
one means or other, become considerable both
for number and riches, and well able to support their own ministers; the Society have still
continued to pay these out of their charitable
fund. The only reason why I do not come to
particulars here, is, lest it should seem too invidious. This conduct of the Society, for some
years proved no inconsiderable means of increasing the church-party : I mean, till a law
of this province was made, obliging the episco-

H   palians,

† A cant term well understood among us.

palians to pay minifterial rates in common with
other people; the money levied on them, however, to go to the fupport of *their own clergy.*
This law feemed to give fome check to the
progrefs of epifcopacy, and a zeal for the
liturgy, in New-England. And if there had
been no fuch act, or the epifcopalians had been
exempted from all minifterial taxes, as the
Quakers are, almoft all who loved their money
better than *any thing elfe,* might in the courfe
of a few years have declared themfelves for,
and adorned the communion of the church—
But this is not defigned as a general reflexion
on the people of that communion here; fome
of whom are doubtlefs perfons of principle,
and fincere piety.

✾✾✾✾✾✾✾✾✾✾✾✾✾✾✾✾✾✾✾✾✾✾✾✾✾✾

SECTION VII.

*The manner in which epifcopal churches
have often fprung up in New-England,
illuftrated and exemplified in a letter of
the late Rev. Dr. COLMAN of Bofton
to Dean, afterwards Bifhop KENNET;
with part of the Dean's anfwer.* †

IT may perhaps be lefs invidious to exemplify fome things in the foregoing fection, relative to the epifcopal churches and miffions
in

† The letters from which thefe extracts are made, are contained at large in the life of Dr. *Colman,* by the Reverend
E. *Turell,* A. M. paftor of *Medford,* p. 122····132.

in New-England, by fome extracts from a letter
of Dr. COLMAN to Dr. KENNET, then Dean
of Peterborough, than by giving any more re-
cent inftances, however notorious.   It was in
1712, that the letter from which the following
extracts are made, was written by the former to
the latter of thofe worthy Divines.

      ' Rev. Sir,   Bofton, Nov. 1712.
  ' I AM altogether a *ftranger* to you, and muft
' needs be *unknown* ; for my name is much too
' *little* to have been heard of by perfons of your
' *dignity* in the eftablifhed church.   But meet-
' ing with your excellent *fermon* preached be-
' fore the honourable and moft reverend *Society*
' ——I cannot forbear afking your leave to
' write you my thoughts upon an admirable
' paffage I find therein, p. 22.

    " NEITHER our *own* people in thofe parts,
" nor their African *flaves*, nor their *Indian*
" neighbours have ought to accufe us of.   At
" leaft we have given no juft *offence* to the *Gen-*
" *tiles* there, nor to the church of God.   We
" truft we have not finned againft the *brethren*,
" and have walked honeftly toward them that
" are without.   We give our money, our at-
" tendance, our correfpondence, our feveral forts
" of care, pains and trouble : Forgive us this
" wrong : If we have done any other, God do
" fo to us, and more alfo."

    ' SIR, there is fuch an air of *fincerity* in thefe
' words, that I cannot but have a perfect *efteem*
' of the good, and truly noble fpirit breathed in
' them.   I doubt not but you fully believe as
               H 2   ' you

‘ you ſpeak, and are accepted by God in your
‘ pious deſires of ſerving the intereſts of religion
‘ in theſe remote parts of the earth.   I greatly
‘ honor the *intentions* of your moſt honourable
‘ Society, their abundant labors and expence.

‘ A MORE noble charity never was projected
‘ than your ſending the *goſpel* among the *hea-*
‘ *then* here, and into *heatheniſh* places, where
‘ the ſettlements have been made void of the
‘ form of religion.   The *harveſt* of this nature
‘ is too plentious thro’ *Virginia, Maryland,* the
‘ *Jerſies,* our *Eaſtern* country alſo, and the *Nar-*
‘ *raganſett,* and ſome places about *Rhode-Iſland,*
‘ which have been too long *neglected,* and ſuf-
‘ fered to run wild into *ſectaries,* and prejudicies
‘ againſt any miniſtry of the word at all.

‘ THIS *vaſt* and *waſte* ſpace, deſolate and pe-
‘ riſhing, cries aloud to you for your charitable
‘ care: And verily the *fund* which the Society
‘ has contributed and gathered is but too little
‘ yet by far, for theſe neceſſitous places; while
‘ at the ſame time many of your miſſions into
‘ our parts, are unto places where the goſpel is
‘ received and preached, and churches gathered
‘ in very good order and manner.——I cannot
‘ but let you know my thoughts, that the reve-
‘ rend and honourable Society have been once
‘ and again miſled, and even impoſed on by
‘ miſ-informations, and private deſigns and in-
‘ tereſts, of perſons and parties here, to miſ-
‘ ſpend (and ſo neceſſarily pervert) great portions
‘ of their noble charity, to ſuch *ends* and in
‘ ſuch *manner* as do not at all anſwer the *pro-*
‘   *pagation*

' *pagation of the gospel* among us, but which do
' really break in upon and hinder the spreading
' and success of it. To evince which, I will
' fairly put the case, and offer an instance or two.

' You must give me leave, Sir, to suppose a
' *town* and *towns* here, wherein *religion* is
' settled, *ministers* legally fixed, the word of God
' faithfully *preached*, and the *sacraments* of
' Christ administred; and yet there happen a
' discontented person· or two in the place; or
' some difference about the placing a new *house*
' for public worship, or about paying their little
' *rate* to the ministry, or the like: Immediately
' they are advised, or in their own mind they
' propose to themselves, "Let us send over to
" the *Lord bishop of London*, or to the honour-
" able Society for propagating the gospel, for a
" minister of the church of England! He will
" bring a salary of £50 sterling"—Now suppose,
' Sir, they actually send and obtain, I demand,
' whether it be not a real injury and *abuse* of
' the Society and their charity; their declared
' end, and the proper *use* of so *great a gift* as
' fifty pound *per annum* is?—Yet are there se-
' veral such notorious instances in our *New-*
' *English provinces*. One was lately in the
' town of *Braintree*, within ten miles of *Boston*,
' which *application* to you the Rev. Mr. *Miles*
' of *Boston* refused to countenance; and was
' free to say, that were the circumstances of the
' place known, my Lord of *London* and the
' Society would never approve of it: For it is
' a notorious matter of fact, that setting aside
' *two*

' *two families* in that party at *Braintree*, the reft
' neither *know why* they fought the *church wor-*
' *fhip* there, nor could be any *credit* to it. Their
' number was fo very *minute*, and their cha-
' racter fo very *mean*, that when a minifter was
' fent to them, he was *afhamed* of his errand,
' and diverted to fome other place of fervice.

' THIS laft year a difference happened in the
' town of *Newbury* about placing their *meeting-*
' *houfe* : The matter was brought before our
' *general court*, who determined it according to
' the free vote and act of the *precinct*, whereby
' they had obliged themfelves to each other.
' Whereupon a number of them declare them-
' felves for the *church of England* ; many of
' them, I will fuppofe, perfons of fobriety and
' virtue, only in a *pet*, and to fave their *rate* to
' their aged and worthy minifter, Mr. Belcher ;
' utterly *ignorant* of the church they declare for,
' nor *offended* in the leaft with the form of wor-
' fhip or dicipline which they turn from ;—be-
' ing till now among the moft *narrow* and *rigid*
' diffenters.——

' IN fhort, Sir, there is a *fordid motive* which
' will find you *beggars* enough for your charity
' in our country-towns ! if you will free them
' from *rates* to any miniftry, and *maintain* it for
' them——You will beft judge, Sir, if there be
' no *offence* to the church of God, in the fteps
' taken by too many, *here* and *there*.'——

THE worthy Dean wrote a very obliging anfwer to the foregoing. His letter is dated Sept.
15. 1713 : In which are the following paffages.
'Rev.

' Rev. Sir,

' Tho' I feem *negligent* in my due acknow-
' ledgment of yours of *Nov.* 1712, yet among
' private friends I have often expreffed my *fatis-*
' *faction* in the fenfe, ftile and temper of it; and
' I now heartily accept fuch a correfpondence,
' and wifh the continuance of it, for the fake of
' our *common caufe* of charity to fouls, and zeal
' to our *Chriftian religion.*

' I was under a great temptation of *communi-*
' *cating* your letter to a *general meeting* of our
' Society; that I might have their *inftructions* for
' an anfwer to the particulars contained in it.——
' But then I thought my felf *reftrained* by fome
' *prudent* intimations of your own; and I was
' very unwilling to draw you into any contro-
' verfy or envy, that two often attend us for
' fpeaking PLAIN TRUTHS: For SUCH indeed
' I believe are the kind informations you give
' me relating to the *places* you mention——It
' is poffible we are not fo intent upon our bufi-
' nefs, *as if it were for filthy lucre*——We are
' lefs *exact* in our correfpondence and *accounts,*
' than if the dear liberty and property *of this*
' *world* depended on it—However, our general
' aim is, to purfue our general commiffion of
' *planting chriftianity* according to the church of
' England, in thofe parts of our Englifh plantati-
' ons, *where there is no fettled miniftry:* or,' &c.——

AFTRR fpeaking of the difficulties which the
Society were under, in refpect of their diftance
from America, the difagreement of accounts
from hence, and expreffing fome hope that the
time

time would come, when the Engliſh in America
ſhould be ' all of *one heart*, and *one way of diſ-*
' *cipline* and *worſhip*,' with ſeveral other particulars, the Dean concludes his letter in the
friendly and catholic manner following—' Our
' exchanging, Sir, the good offices of common
' charity and a public ſpirit, will help much, un-
' der Gᴏᴅ's bleſſing, to *enlarge* our underſtand-
' ings and our affections alſo to each other; and
' ſo to meet *nearer* upon earth, and *inſeperably*
' in heaven. Let theſe be our mutual prayers
' and endeavours. I am, dear Sir, your affec-
' tionate *Friend* and *Brother*,

WʜɪᴛE KEɴɴEᴛ.

Now, the manner in which epiſcopal churches
have been founded in the Maſſachuſetts and
Connecticut, has all along in general borne but
too near a reſemblance to that repreſented in
Dr. Cᴏʟᴍᴀɴ's letter aforeſaid: And the worthy Dean was ſo juſt as to expreſs his intire be-
lief of what the Dr. ſaid *relating to the places*
which he mentioned ; ſuppoſing theſe repreſentations to be ſome of thoſe *plain truths,* which
too often draw people into *controverſy* and *envy.*
He alſo ſpeaks of it as the primary deſign of the
Society's inſtitution, to plant epiſcopal churches
' in thoſe parts of our Engliſh plantations, where
' there is *no ſettled miniſtry ;*' tho' not exclu-
ſively of thoſe, where there are '. *good num-*
' *bers* who cannot *in conſcience* conform to the
' ways of worſhip different from the eſtabliſhed
' church' of England. The invalidity of which
plea of *conſcience,* as it relates to the preſent controverſy, will be ſhewn hereafter.

SECTION

SECTION VIII.

That the aforesaid Conduct of the Society *is not agreeable to the Letter or Spirit of their Charter.*

SUPPOSING the truth of the *principal* facts reprefented in the foregoing fections; particularly as to the ftate of religion in New-England, the number of miffionaries, &c. maintained here by the Society, and the places in which they are fupported; which I confider as the *principal* facts, even in diftinction from the *difhonourable manner* in which epifcopal parties have often arofe, been encouraged and increafed here; (which is confidered only as an incidental circumftance, not a principal fact, upon which the argument finally turns) Suppofing the truth of thofe facts, I fay, almoft any unprejudiced perfon may eafily fee, that fuch a conduct in the Society is not conformable to their charter in any one material circumftance, but effentially repugnant thereto. The contraft, or the oppofition betwixt the charter and fuch a conduct, may be made to appear in a very few words.

1. IT is allowed on all hands, that one material end of this inftitution, according to the charter, was, *propagating the gofpel* among the *heathen* bordering on the Britifh plantations. But no one will pretend to fay, that the miffionaries in New-England are employed directly in *that good work.*

I   2. ANOTHER

2. ANOTHER end was, the maintaining a public worſhip in thoſe colonies, where the people, tho' called Chriſtians, were " *wholly* " deſtitute and unprovided,"——where they " wanted the adminiſtration of God's word and " ſacraments, and ſeemed to be abandoned to " *atheiſm* and infidelity," &c. But, that this neither is, nor ever was, the true ſtate of New-England, at leaſt not of the Maſſachuſetts and Connecticut, is ſufficiently apparent.

3. ANOTHER end of the inſtitution, which is indeed the firſt mentioned in the charter, was, the benefit and aſſiſtance of thoſe plantations, in which, tho' there were ſuch miniſters as are deſigned in the charter, yet there was not a tolerable or competent proviſion made for their ſubſiſtence; or, in the words of the charter, in which the proviſion made for them was " very mean." Whereas it is a known fact, that in moſt of thoſe places in New-England where the ſociety ſupport miſſions, there was a legal and competent proviſion before made for the ſupport of an " able, learned, orthodox miniſtry."

4 .THESE three are the *only* ends of the inſti-tution expreſly mentioned in, or that can fairly be inferred from the charter of the Society. And conſequently, if they have annually expended a large ſum here in New-England, not conforma-bly to either of them, this muſt needs be a miſ-application. Whatever they have expended, more or leſs, to accompliſh ends different from theſe, or ſuch as are not directly ſubſervient to them, has been laid out in a manner not warranted
by

by the charter; and therefore perverted and alienated from the true, important ends of their inftitution. Let the knowing and impartial judge, whether this conclufion is fairly drawn or not, fuppofing the truth of the facts aforefaid; which are indeed too notorious to admit of a denial.

✿✿✿✿✿✿✿✿✿✿✿✿✿✿✿✿✿✿✿✿✿✿✿✿✿✿

SECTION IX.

Of Objections againft the Reafoning in the preceeding Sections; and particularly as to a learned *and* orthodox *Miniftry.*

IF the facts aforefaid are allowed, no *folid objection*, it is conceived, can be brought againft the general conclufion as to the perverfion or mifapplication of the Society's charity; tho' a perfon who fets himfelf to invent *evafions*, may poffibly think of a number of *weak* ones. And the ingenious Mr. *Apthorp* has been fo lucky as to hit upon feveral fuch in his *Confiderations*, defigned to vindicate the Society againft that charge, which has often been brought againft their conduct in refpect of New-England. One of thefe evafions has already been hinted at: But it may be proper to fpeak of it a little more diftinctly, tho' briefly, here—It is faid, the minifters fpoken of in the charter, are fpoken of under the defignation of " learned and orthodox."

Now.

Now, as to *learning* ; tho' the minifters educated in our young, but growing Colleges in New-England, may not vie with this gentleman, who brought with him the *advantageous* reputation of a confiderable Scholar from one of the ancient and renowned Britifh Univerfities, in which, it is faid, he reaped fome laurels ;—a reputation which he doubtlefs merited; yet, as the truly knowing and learned, are generally *candid* alfo, it is hoped that he will not abfolutely deny *that qualification* to our clergy, in the degree neceffary to render them ufeful and fufficient minifters, provided they are not defective in the other material point, *orthodoxy*. And, to do the gentleman juftice, he feems wholly to wave the former, and to deny our clergy *nothing but orthodoxy ;* in which, other people generally fuppofe, they are not deficient. After mentioning it as the primary defign of the inftitution aforefaid, to " provide a maintenance for an or-
" thodox clergy ;" he fubjoins, " which (as the
" charter was obtained by the members of the
" church of England) muft, in all reafonable
" conftruction, mean a clergy of their own
" church. '† So that, there being no fuch minifters amongft *Us*, in the fenfe of the charter, it was incumbent upon the Society to fupply Bofton, Cambridge, &c. &c. with *orthodox* miffionaries: in doing which, they conform to the original and *charitable* defign of their inftitution.   This is the obvious intent of what the gentleman fays upon this head ; tho', for certain prudential reafons, he did not chufe, in a more explicit man-

ncr,

† *Confid.* p. 11.

ner, to monopolize *all the orthodoxy* in New-England to himself, the other missionaries, and the people of the church of England ; stigmatizing all our ministers and churches as *heretical* or *unorthodox*. This is indeed the unavoidable consequence of his appropriating and confining the terms *orthodox ministers*, to those of the episcopal communion. But, to have reproached us thus in plain words, might have been a *bolder* stroke than the *times* would well bear as yet; and so, rather prejudiced than served the cause in which he engaged. This might perhaps have contributed to frustrate the modest hopes which he expressed of great accessions to the episcopal party at Cambridge, in his letter to the Society soon after his mission there, dated Aug. 30. 1760. some time before the church was " fit for di-" vine service." For it is said in the *abstract* printed in 1761, that Mr. *Apthorp* had written, that the " building of the church was in such " forwardness, that he hoped it would be fit for " divine service in *November ;* and particular " care had been taken to make the structure use-" ful and durable, as well as decently elegant ; " and, in case of *future accessions* to the congre-" gation, it might be *easily enlarged;* and he " had the satisfaction to add, that it *already pro-*" *mised* to be one of the *best supported*, and " *most flourishing churches in* America."† It would doubtless be a great pity that the gentleman's wishes and expectations should prove abortive, if there is no *orthodox* minister in Cambridge besides himself, tho' there are three

of

† *Abstract*, 1761. p. 44, 45.

of our congregational churches, as well as the College, in that town.

BUT the following conſiderations, ſome of which were before hinted at, (p. 21) will be ſufficient to ſhew that our miniſters are not deſtitute of *orthodoxy,* altho' they are not conformiſts to the church of England; and that the gentleman is a little too ſelfiſh, in endeavouring to engroſs the whole of that precious *commodity* to himſelf and his party. Tho' if *orthodoxy* has the property which an eminent divine of the church of England ‡ ſarcaſtically aſcribes to it,—that of "covering a multitude of ſins," I will not deny, but yet do not affirm, that they have rather more *occaſion* for it than thoſe whom they would ſtrip of it, leaving them nothing *better* than *charity* to ſupply its place—

ORTHODOXY, in the commonly-received ſenſe of the word amongſt proteſtants at leaſt, notwithſtanding its general etemology, relates particularly to doctrinal points, or articles of faith, as diſtinguiſhed from opinions about the beſt modes of eccleſiaſtic polity, external order, rites and ceremonies. To theſe latter it has no reference in its moſt common uſe. And it can hardly be ſuppoſed, that a gentleman ſo well ſkilled in Chriſtian philology as Mr. *Apthorp,* will diſpute this point.

FROM whence it follows, that miniſters or churches differing widely in opinion about an hierarchy, diſcipline, and modes of worſhip, may yet be equally orthodox; agreeing nearly in the ſame common faith reſpecting GOD, JESUS CHRIST, his offices and redemption.   IT

‡ Bp. HARE, *Difficulties* and *Diſcouragements,* &c.

IT is alfo a known fact, that the minifters and churches in New-England, with a very few exceptions, if any, agree in doctrinal points, and therefore in refpect of orthodoxy, with the church of England, according to her articles relative to thefe points.

IT is moreover known, or at leaft generally fuppofed amongft us, that our New-England minifters, a very few excepted, adhere much more clofely in their preaching, both to the letter and fpirit of thofe doctrinal articles, than moft of the epifcopal clergy themfelves, whether here or in England. And if this be fact, as I am fully perfuaded it is, the former are really *more* orthodox than the latter, even according to the articles of their own church. Befides:

BY the fame rule that this gentleman and fome others deny our minifters the title of orthodox, limiting it to the " clergy of their own church;" they muft deny it to the minifters of the eftablifhed church of Scotland, and of all other churches, except perhaps that of Rome. For none of them fully agree with the church of England, except in doctrinal points, as we alfo do; which, it feems, is not fufficient to denominate them orthodox. According to which pretence, there will be no orthodox minifters in the world, except of the church of England: And is not this very modeft and candid !

DIVERS of *our* laws relative to minifters, and in which they are defigned as orthodox, having had the allowance of the King, the head of the Englifh church, this feems to be a royal acknowledgment

knowledgment of their orthodoxy. And is it not somewhat presumptuous for any of the members of that body to contradict their head!

NOTWITHSTANDING those ministers and churches in England, with which ours in New-England very nearly agree in doctrine, discipline and worship, have often been accused by the episcopalians as *schismatical*, on account of their dissent from the church there established; yet they have not often been reproached as heterodox, heretical or un-orthodox in that respect. So far from it, that I do not think there can be a single episcopal divine of reputation produced, or other approved writer on that side within a century past, who has taxed them in a body as heretics, or denied them to be orthodox, on account of their non-conformity. Mr. *Apthorp* seems to have forgotten that the episcopal divines in England, even in their highest flights, have generally distinguished betwixt heterodoxy and schism; while he, it seems, is for confounding them together, and will not allow us to be orthodox even in New-England, unless we will become conformists to a church that is not established here.

IT has before been observed, how unnatural it is to suppose that King WILLIAM designed to limit the terms "orthodox ministers" in the charter, to those of the church of England; and thereby to brand the ministers of all other protestant churches as heterodox; which were to suppose that catholic-spirited Prince as great a bigot as any of his royal predecessors.

BESIDES:

BESIDES : The whole air and complexion of the charter are catholic in the higheſt degree : There is no hint or alluſion therein as to any differences amongſt proteſtants. The grand end propoſed therein, is propagating the *goſpel*, the principles of *true religion*, and the *Chriſtian religion*, in oppoſition to *atheiſm*, *infidelity* and *popery* : And orthodox miniſters ſtand there in direct oppoſition to popiſh prieſts and jeſuits ; as before obſerved. It is therefore contrary to all the rules of good criticiſm, as well as to catholic chriſtianity, to appropriate and confine theſe terms to the miniſters of the church of England, and thereby to hereticate the miniſters of all other proteſtant churches. Nothing can be leſs conformable to the language, and whole ſpirit of the charter.

IF this argument of Mr. *Apthorp* were of any force, it is not eaſy to ſee why the Society might not ſend miſſionaries into Scotland to convert the kirk to epiſcopacy, by virtue of their charter, as well as into New-England, to convert us ; excepting only that Scotland is not a " plantation, colony or factory beyond ſeas ;" and, in that reſpect, certainly not within the deſign of the charter.

THIS point may be now diſmiſſed with reminding the reader of the reply of Mr. HOBART to ſome of his antagoniſts, relative thereto. " If," ſaid he, " they think that none but the " clergy of the church of England are in a legal " ſenſe *orthodox* miniſters, Dr. MACSPARRAN " can inform them how that matter was deter-

K   " mined

" mined by the King in council, in the caſe
" between him and Mr. Torrey.†" ‡

SECTION

† *Second Addreſs, p.* 143.

‡ Some of the more bigotted ſort of epiſcopalians amongſt us,
ſcruple not to ſay boldly and plumply, that we have no
goſpel-miniſters at all ; no ſacraments, or goſpel-ordinances,
nor any chriſtian churches ; for this goodly reaſon, that our
miniſters have not had epiſcopal ordination after the mode
of the church of England. Where they learn this ſilly
cant, it is not worth while to enquire. I am not willing
to impute ſuch pitiful conceits to the ingenious Mr.
Apthorp ; eſpecially ſince his anonimous friend in the
piece dated at Cambridge the 25th March laſt, and publiſhed in the New-England *Chronicle,* ſpeaks of him as
no bigot, but a catholic-ſpirited gentleman ;---as one who is
" ſo far from thinking every punctilio in the modes of wor-
" ſhip eſtabliſhed in the church of England, *jure divino,*
" that he makes no ſcruple to confeſs even to thoſe who ſe-
" cede from her, that he is of opinion no particular mode
" of worſhip can be preciſely aſcertained from any thing re-
" revealed in the new teſtament, and that therefore mutual
" forbearance ought to be exerciſed in this reſpect ."-----
as one " publickly averring he deſired not *to make one pro-*
" *ſelyte from the congregational* church ;"-----and "keep-
" ing up a friendly interchange of viſits with its pastor"
---There ſeems, however, to be ſome difficulty in reconciling this declaration, that he *deſires not to make one proſelyte
from the congregational church,* with the hopes expreſſed in
his letter to the Society, of *future acceſſions to his own congregation ;* ſo that there might be occaſion for *enlarging* the
church, &c. (ſee before, p. 69.) But perhaps it was from
the College only, not from the congregational church at
Cambridge, that he flattered himſelf with ſuch large *accef-
ſions* to the ſmall epiſcopal party there. In which reſpect
the gentleman is ſuppoſed to have been not a little diſ-
appointed-----

☞ There is a chronological miſtake in the margin of p. 52.
which the author takes this firſt opportunity to correct, after
the diſcovery---It was not in the reign of *James* II. and adminiſtration of Sir *E. Andros,* that the Biſhop of London
prevailed with the King to allow an epiſcopal church in
Boſton ; but in the reign of *Charles* II. when Mr. *S. Brad-
ſtreet* was Governor here, *An.* 1679.

SECTION X.

The Plea of Conscience, *as it relates to the present Question, considered.*

BY way of answer to the objection so often made against the Society's conduct in supporting missions in those colonies, where the people " have the means of religion already, " in other protestant communions ;" Mr. *Apthorp* says, " This is not universally true : or " wherever it happily is true; this brings us " back to the claim of liberty of *conscience*. The " means of religion are NO MEANS to him whose " *conscience* cannot use, or does not approve " them: no more than Popery or Mahometa- " nism afford the means of religion to a good " Protestant, who happens to reside in Popish " or Mahometan countries."† Something of this sort has been said in divers of the anniversary sermons before the Society: And Mr. *Apthorp* might perhaps take the hint from that excellent Prelate " who now so worthily *presides* " *over the church of England,*" [I hope he meant in subordination to the King] " AND " THE SOCIETY ITSELF ;" *(Conf.* p. 19.) This great Prelate, a distinguished member of the Society, is one of the two witnesses whom Mr. *Apthorp* summons to bear " testimony" in favor of the Society, after producing that of

K 2 Bishop

† *Consid.* p. 14.

Bifhop BERKLEY, another member of the Society, in this caufe. Speaking of whom con-
junctly, he fays, he " confidently refts his *proof*
" on the unexceptionable teftimony of two moft
" candid and truly Chriftian Prelates," &c.
(p. 18.) The teftimony of the worthy Bifhop
BERKLEY has already been taken notice of.
The other of thefe witneffes is quoted by Mr.
Apthorp as having given an anfwer fimilar to
his own, to the objection aforefaid, in the following words—" An objection to the conduct
" of the Society, is that they have fent miffiona-
" ries to fome places in which there were alrea-
" dy Chriftian affemblies eftablifhed and fup-
" ported. But in the *left* exceptionable of *thefe*
" *affemblies*, there are feveral things, which the
" *confciences* of many (we apprehend, with great
" reafon) cannot acquiefce in ; who were not
" therefore to be left deftitute of public worfhip ;
" efpecially as our charter was granted in exprefs
" terms, *for the maintenance of an* orthodox
" *clergy in thofe parts.*"† So that, it feems, one
material point which his GRACE is called to
bear teftimony to, is, that the *confciences* of many people in thefe parts, cannot *acquiefce* in feveral things found even in *the leaft exceptionable*
of our Chriftian affemblies, &c. Let me make a
few remarks upon the foregoing paffage in the
Confiderations, thus fupported by the *teftimony*
of this great Prelate. And,

1. MR. *Apthorp* plainly allows that the people in fome of the colonies have the means of
religion already, without the Society's charity,

in

† *Confid.* p. 21.

in other proteſtant communions ; by ſaying that
*this is not univerſally true ; or wherever it hap-
pily is true,* &c.

2. IF this is *happily true* in any of the American colonies, I conclude he will allow it to be
ſo in this province and in Connecticut, which
have much the faireſt pretenſions to ſuch a pre-
eminence ; and to the proceedings of the Society in which, the objection principally relates.
It is therefore conceived, that it may be naturally taken as a conceſſion of Mr. *Apthorp,* that
in theſe principal parts of New-England, where
ſo many epiſcopal miſſions have been ſupported
by the Society, the inhabitants had the means
of religion already, *in other proteſtant communions.*

3. THEREFORE, according to the reaſoning
in the preceeding ſections, which needs not to
be here repeated, theſe are not *ſuch* colonies as
were the proper objects of that charity : For
their ſtate in reſpect of religion, is eſſentially different from that of the places deſcribed in the
charter; and for which a charitable proviſion
was made thereby. So that the money expended
here by the Society as aforeſaid, is not employed in conformity to the true intent of the charter : For who can, with the leaſt appearance of
reaſon, ſay, that the charter makes proviſion for
thoſe plantations, in which the people enjoyed
the means of religion already, in ANY *proteſtant
communion ?*—thoſe in which a ſufficient number of proteſtant miniſters of ANY denomination
were competently provided for, and God's public worſhip was conſtantly upheld ?

4. As

4. As to the plea of *conscience*, that there are some persons amongst us, who cannot use the means of religion, which they have in our *protestant communions*; and that to such persons these are NO MEANS, any more than Popery or Mahometanism, &c: If these very conscientious people were as entirely protestant in their sentiments, as our communions are in their nature, it might perhaps in part remove the difficulty. What there is in the least exceptionable of our truly Christian and protestant assemblies, which should give offence to the consciences of sincere, good protestants, neither Mr. *Apthorp* nor his GRACE has particularly declared: Whether it be the preaching, so strictly agreeable in general to the doctrinal articles of the church of England; or the devout prayers, not read to GOD, but dictated by the heart, as in the truly primitive and apostolic churches; or the administration of the sacraments in the most simple and scriptural manner, without any of those additions which the wisdom of the clergy afterwards invented; or whether it be any thing else, we are left to conjecture; and so cannot particularly answer this objection against our *protestant communions*, as Mr. *Apthorp*, or *Christian assemblies*, as his GRACE is pleased to call them. It seems they both decline giving these the name of *churches*: But for what reason, it is not easy to say. It is to be hoped, they can form some idea of a truly christian and protestant church, without a King or Queen at its head; without numerous acts of parliament to model

its

its conftitution, and eftablifh its ceremonials; without printed forms of devotion ; and without an hierarchy refembling that of the Romifh church, in which *one* great Prelate *prefides* over the whole, with all the inferior religious orders, the loweft of which are as it were trodden in the dirt ;—an hierarchy which, in a word, may be compared to Jacob's ladder,

"Its foot on earth, its top above the fkies."

If there are any perfons amongft us, who have no conceptions of a truly Chriftian church, but in connexion with fuch things as thefe, it is not indeed ftrange that the means of public religion which they might have in our *proteftant communions*, fhould be no means to them ; or that their confciences fhould not fully *acquiefce* in them ; not even fo readily as they might in *Popery*. Indeed I have myfelf heard fome epifcopalians amongft us, who were reckoned very good church-men, fay, that they fhould much prefer the *communion* of the church of Rome to ours ; and would fooner go to mafs than come to our affembles, if there were here any Romifh, and no Englifh churches. This I declare, of my own certain knowledge, and could mention names ; and I have divers times heard credible perfons fpeak of fome *confcientious* epifcopalians amongft us, as expreffing themfelves after the fame manner : Tho', to do them juftice, I do not fuppofe that thefe fentiments generally prevail amongft them. Some of them may *poffibly*, without going thefe lengths, have confcientious fcruples about the means of religion in our *proteftant*

teftant communions : But to fay, that becaufe there are fome things or circumftances attending them, which they cannot intirely *acquiefce* in, or *approve* of, therefore they are abfolutely NO MEANS at all to them, is at beft a very extraordinary pofition.   However,

5. IT is readily granted, that great allowances ought to be made for *weak* and *fcrupulous, tender,* and even *erroneous* confciences ; and for the prejudices of education, in matters merely of a religious nature.   And this plea of confcience ought to be allowed valid thus far, *viz.* That thefe confcientious people among us, fhould not be *compelled* to join in our *proteftant communion ;* but left intirely at liberty to worfhip GOD according to the epifcopal mode, even tho' we may think it confiderably lefs proteftant and fcriptural than our own.   Indeed there are not a few of them, whom we fhould be far from *defiring* to fee coming to *our communion,* unlefs they were much more *confcientious* in fome other refpects, than they appear to be— The government here neither pretends nor defires to deprive them of their religious liberty : Tho' by the way, had the government in England allowed our Fore-fathers the like liberty of confcience, they would have had no occafion to take refuge in New-England, from their fufferings for non-conformity.   BUT,

6. How good a plea foever this of confcience may be for liberty, in oppofition to all *reftraint* or *conftraint* in matters purely religious; yet it feems far from a folid one as ufed by his

GRACE

Grace the Arch-bishop of Canterbury, and Mr. *Apthorp*, in order to juftify the Society in the application of fo much of their money, or even any part of it, for the fupport and increafe of the epifcopal party among us. The reafon is obvious from what has been faid before : Their whole fund and revenue are *otherwife appropriated* by their charter itfelf ; *viz.* to the propagating the gofpel among the heathen, and to the maintenance of God's public worfhip in thofe plantations, in which no competent provifion was before made for minifters ; and in which the people, for want of the means of religion in any proteftant cammunion, feem'd abandoned to atheifm and infidelity, or in imminent danger of being perverted to popery. To alienate their revenue from *thefe* important ends, under a pretence of gratifying fome *fcrupulous confciences*, in places where a legal and competent provifion was before made for the maintenance of minifters, and a public, proteftant religion ; is a manifeft abufe and perverfion of that charity, even upon fuppofition that thefe confcientious people among us were much to be pitied, and really the objects of charity. If any perfons in England, in their private capacity, fhould think it a deed of charity to advance money for fupporting epifcopal churches here, for the fake of thofe comparatively few *confcientious* people, to whom the means of religion which are to be had in our proteftant communions, are NO MEANS at all, any more than Popery or Mahometanifm ;

L   they

they have an undoubted right to do it. But the caſe of the Society is eſſentially different in this reſpect, from that of private perſons : They have not the ſame right to diſpoſe of their money, that a private man has to diſpoſe of his property ; the former being particularly appropriated to certain uſes and ends, from which it may not be alienated to any others, even tho' good in themſelves.

THAT argument which Mr. *Apthorp* quotes from the great Prelate aforeſaid ;— that " the charter was granted in expreſs terms, for the maintenance of an *orthodox* clergy" in the colonies ; cannot be thought one of his GRACE's " invincible reaſons" which Mr. *Apthorp* ſpeaks of, till it is proved that no clergymen beſides thoſe of the church of England, can properly be called *orthodox* miniſters, even tho' they adhere to the doctrinal articles of that church more cloſely than her own clergy. But enough of this before. And the intelligent reader is now left to judge, whether Mr. *Apthorp* had reaſon to uſher in his *two witneſſes,* as he does in the following words— " To take leave of this po-
" pular objection with *ſo full a confutation,* that
" it will be *diſingenuous* ever to advance it again ;
" the writer *confidently reſts his proof on the*
" *unexceptionable teſtimony*", &c. † That he does this *confidently,* no one will deny ; but that theſe teſtimonies are ſo intirely *unexceptionable* in this cauſe, as to be a juſt ground for ſuch confidence,

is

† *Conſideration,* p. 18.

is far lefs apparent ;—efpecially confidered as teftimonies of the party *accufed*. But yet it is not eafy to fee, why he might not call in the Society as witneffes in their own caufe, with as much propriety at leaft, as he had before fubmitted his defence of them to their *own judgment and decifion.* One of the witneffes, however, bifhop BERKLEY, fays nothing directly to the main point, as to the miffions in thofe colonies wherein proteftant churches were *before fettled :* The other, his GRACE of *Canterbury*, does ; but yet perhaps not fo convincingly, as to render it quite *difingenuous ever to advance this objection again.*

✻✻✻✻✻✻✻✻✻✻✻✻✻✻✻✻✻✻✻✻✻✻✻✻

SECTION XI.

Of the great Good which Mr. Apthorp *fuppofes the Society have done by their Miffionaries, in bettering the general State of Religion among us.*

UPON this head the ingenious gentleman expreffes himfelf thus. " That the ftate " of religion among ourfelves is now *fo much* " *fuperior* to what it was, when the miffions " were firft appointed, is, under God, *fo greatly* " *the work of the Society*, that to give this rea- " fon for their with-holding their protection

" from

" from our churches, is to make the ſucceſs and
" benefit of their deſign, an argument againſt
" it †".

1. WHO ever *gave* this *reaſon for their with-
holding their protection from the epiſcopal churches here*, that the ſtate of religion among ourſelves *is now ſo much ſuperior to what it was*,
&c ? They muſt be ſtrange objectors indeed,
who could object after this manner ; which is
the plain import of Mr. *Apthorp*'s words. And
one may be confident, without preſumption, that
no perſon among us ever objected againſt the
Society's conduct, or their miſſionaries, that the
ſtate of religion among us *is much ſuperior* to
what it was formerly ; tho'. many have objected
the direct contrary.

2. As to the important fact which Mr. *Apthorp* ſuppoſes, viz. that the ſtate of religion
here is much *ſuperior* to what it formerly was ;
many perſons who were men of obſervation before either Mr. *Apthorp* or I was born ; who
have always lived, and ſtill are living in the
country, will by no means agree with him. In
their opinion, the general ſtate of religion in
this country, is not ſo good as it was " when.
the miſſions were firſt appointed in it;" tho' I
will not myſelf aſſert any thing poſitively upon
this head.   But,

3. THO' this fact were certainly true ; yet it
is by no means a clear point, that this reformation is *ſo greatly the work of the Society* or their
miſſionaries,

† *Conſiderations*, p. 17.

miffionaries, as he is pleafed, in his great civility
to them, to take for granted. I might engage
to bring twenty perfons who think the religious
ftate of the country worfe than it was, and who
attribute this in a great meafure to the *fame caufe*
to which he afcribes the reformation of it, for
one that he can produce to fupport his double
hypothefis. But fuppofing the reformation real ;
yet there is no reafon to think that this is *great-*
ly the work of the Society, if at all.

4. SUPPOSING the truth of both thefe facts ;
yet this will not juftify the Society in a *mifap-*
plication of monies entrufted with them ; and
neglecting thofe places which were the direct,
proper objects of their charity, according to the
charter. To plead the good done in fuch a
cafe as this, however undifputed ; tho' it may be
confidered as fome apology for, yet it cannot be
confidered as a proper vindication of, thofe who
did it ; efpecially if it has occafioned the neglect
of a much greater good to the heathens, or to
thofe colonies wherein no tolerable provifion
was made for the adminiftration of God's word
and facraments. This plea is as invalid, as if,
when a particular perfon is accufed of mifapply-
ing the money put into his hands exprefly for
the ufe of A, perifhing with hunger and cold ; it
fhould be alleged in his vindication, that he had
laid it out for the benefit of B ; and fed and
cloathed him *more elegantly* than he was cloathed
and fed before. How would this excufe him
in leaving A, the intended and proper object of
the

the charity, to periſh for want of thoſe things that are *needful* for the body ? The application is eaſy, and cannot be miſtaken.

✳✳✳✳✳✳✳✳✳✳✳✳✳✳✳✳✳✳✳✳✳✳✳✳✳✳

SECTION XII.

Some farther reflections on the ſame Point, occaſioned by the Conſiderations.

BUT Mr. *Apthorp* deſcends to ſome particulars, in which he ſuppoſes the ſtate of religion among us is greatly improved by the charitable care of the Society. " Every one," ſays he, " who knows the hiſtory of this coun-
" try muſt acknowledge, that the religious ſtate
" of it is manifeſtly improved : *notwithſtanding*
" *the* IMMORALITIES and defects which we
" lament, and wiſh to reform in the preſent
" MANNERS and principles. Religion no lon-
" ger wears among us that *ſavage* and *gloomy*
" *appearance*, with which *ſuperſtition* had terribly
" arrayed *her* : its ſpeculative doctrines are freed
" from thoſe *ſenſeleſs horrors* with which *fanati-*
" *ciſm* had perverted them : *Hypocriſy* has worn
" off, in proportion as men have ſeen the *beauty*
" *of holineſs* : and above all, that exterminating
" monſter *perſecution*, is itſelf exterminated both
" from the temper and practice of the age.
" *Much indeed remains to be done in* MANNERS
" *and* PIETY", &c †. How greatly are we indebted to the Society !   BUT

† *Conſiderations*, p. 17.

But yet here feems to be a conceffion, that the boafted reformation in the ftate of religion among us, very little, if at all confifts in the improvement of our *morals, manners,* and *piety.* It is not pretended by Mr. *Apthorp,* that there has been any confiderable reformation in thefe refpects, fince the miffions were firft appointed here, which is *greatly the work of the Society.*

But

He fays, *Religion no longer wears among us that favage and gloomy appearance,* &c. And, not to difpute with this ingenious gentleman about fmall matters, it fhall be allowed, (if that is what he means) that the *faces* of people in general are lefs *grave* and *folemn* than they were a century ago, or even fince the inftitution of the Society : And this *improvement,* it may alfo be conceded, is *greatly the work of the Society,* by the inftrumentality of thofe good gentlemen the miffionaries, who commonly appear with a pretty gray, debonair and jovial countenance. But it is not quite clear from hence, that *the ftate of religion is now much fuperior to what it was before.* If divers of our Forefathers had fomewhat *too long* faces, and a too fet, formal air ; yet they might be very pious, virtuous and worthy men. And tho I would by no means deny the venerable Society or their miffionaries any praife which may juftly belong to them for contributing to the mirth, gaiety and chearfulnefs of our countenances ; yet methinks the gentleman went a little two far in ufing the expreffion

SAVAGE

SAVAGE *and gloomy appearance ;* partly (unlefs I
miftake his meaning) to exprefs his diflike to the
faces of our good Fathers,fome of whofe pictures
he may probably have feen.   And it may perhaps be worthy of his confideration,whether this
diflike might not in part be owing to the unfkil-
fulnefs of the *painters* of thofe days.   But be
that as it may, it might ftill be worthy of his
confideration, whether, fince the miffionaries
came among us, many people are not run into
an extreme quite oppofite to gloominefs and
precifenefs, and even to that gravity and fobriety
which become the Chriftian character ; putting
on a light, thoughtlefs air and behaviour.   He
will not deny but that people may riot, laugh and
frolick, curfe, fwear and game too much, as well
as wear too grave and formal a countenance.
Thofe are much worfe, and more dangerous extremes than this.   And many perfons that were
men before either of *us* was born, can atteft
that fuch exceffes. are, beyond all comparifon,
more frequent fince the church of England prevailed here, than they were before ; and have increafed in fome proportion to its flourifhing. But,
what the true caufe hereof is, fuppofing the fact,
is another point : And, for my own part, I will
not affirm that this is *greatly the work of the
Society.*

BUT the gentleman intimates, that the ftate of
religion is much improved among us, in refpect
of its fpeculative doctrines, how little foever it
may be in refpect of *manners* and *piety*— *Its
fpeculative*

speculative doctrines, fays he, *are freed from thofe fenfelefs horrors with which fanaticifm had perverted them.* Let it be here obferved,

1. That Mr. *Apthorp* feems not only too harfh, but a little impolitic in giving fuch an account of our Forefathers. He had juft before fpoken of religion among them, as having been *terribly arrayed by fuperftition.* And here they are reprefented as a parcel of wretched *Fanatics,* who had perverted the fpeculative doctrines of religion with *fenfelefs horrors.* Mr. *Apthorp* in his *Confiderations,* (p. 23.) expreffes great indignation at the author of a fuppofed infult on the memory of a deceafed miffionary; which was yet, perhaps, no infult. But whofe memory does this fame gentleman now infult in fo licentious a manner?— In effect, the memory of all the pious Fathers of New-England, fo juftly venerable and dear to their pofterity, whofe faith is in fubftance the fame with their's to this day. So that he does, in a fort, infult the living and the dead at the fame time; and not a few particular perfons only, but the people of a country in general. This, to be fure, does not feem the likelieft way to make profelytes to the church—

2. This outrage is the more to be wondered at, becaufe the gentleman does, by natural implication, infult the Fathers and Founders of his own church at the fame time. For it is a known fact, that the *fpeculative doctrines* almoft univerfally received and pro-

M   feffed

feffed inNew-England from firft to laft, are in effect the fame with thofe of the church of England according to her articles. I fuppofe, with others, that the gentleman had here a more particular view to the Calviniftic doctrines of original fin, juftification by faith alone, election and reprobation. In this fentiment I am confirmed by a paffage in a fermon of Mr. *Apthorp*, publifhed a year or two fince; wherein he exprefies himfelf with fo much contempt and horror of thofe, who " draw portraits of " the DEITY from the fanguinary paffions " of the worft men—reprefenting the all-mer- " ciful Father as the tyrant of the univerfe, " reprobating his creatures, pre-determining " their crimes, and predeftinating their eter- " nal mifery :" of perfons who falfely charge on Chriftianity opinions " fubverfive of all " moral obligation, leading weak minds into " enthufiafm and licentioufnefs "—of perfons by whom " a juft attention to the caufe of " virtue is reproached as derogating from the " glories of HIM, *who hath fanctified us with* " *His blood;* and the juftification of finners— " is propofed in fuch a manner, as to render " virtue ufelefs and even a crime :--thefe hor- " rors," &c.† I believe hardly any one who reads this paffage, will doubt but that the Calviniftic doctrines aforefaid, are thofe to which Mr. *Apthorp* refers in his *Confiderations*, as the *fpeculative doctrines* of our *fuperftiticus, fanatical* Forefathers;

† *The Conftitution of a Chriftian Church,* &c. p. 8. Preached at the Confecration of the new Church in Cambridge.

Forefathers; the effects of which are suppo-
fed to have been, the making them *savage* and
gloomy, and filling them with *senseless horrors.*
I would not be over confident ; but yet take
this to have been his true meaning. And, what
the church of England professes in her articles respecting those doctrines, the reader
may be pleased to see in the margin, where
the substance of several articles is quoted : *

M 2   Whereby

* " ARTICLE IX. *Of original or Birth-Sin.* Original fin
" standeth not in the following of *Adam* (as the Pelagians
" do vainly talk) but it is the fault and corruption of the
" nature of every man —and therefore in every person that
" is born into this world, *it deserveth God's wrath and
" damnation*"—

" ARTICLE XI. *Of the Justification of Man.* We are
" accounted righteous before God, only for the merit of
" our Lord and Saviour Jesus Christ by *faith,* and not for
" our *works* or *deservings* "—

" ARTICLE XIII. *Of Works before Justification.* Works
" done before the grace of Christ, and the inspiration of his
" Spirit, are not *pleasant* to God——yea, rather for that
" they are not done as God hath willed and commanded
" them to be done, we doubt not but that they have *the
" nature of fin.*"

" ARTICLE XVII. *Of Predestination and Election.*
" Predestination to life is the everlasting purpose of God,
" whereby (before the foundations of the world were laid)
" he hath constantly decreed by his counsel, secret to us,
" to deliver from curse and damnation, *those whom he hath
" chosen in Christ out of mankind,* to bring them by Christ
" to everlasting salvation, as vessels made to honor.——As
" the godly consideration of predestination, and our elec-
" tion in Christ, is full of sweet, pleasant, and unspeakable
" comfort to godly persons :——So for curious and carnal per-
" sons, lacking the Spirit of Christ, *to have continually be-
" fore their eyes the sentence of God's predestination,* is a *most
" dangerous downfal,* whereby the Devil doth thrust them
" either into *desparation,* or into wretchlessness of most *un-
" clean living,* no less perilous than *desparation.*"

Whereby one may be the better able to judge of Mr. *Apthorp*'s fincerity and confiftency in fubfcribing thofe articles as part of his faith ; tho' it is indeed poffible that he has altered his opinion fince, as a very honeft man might do.   But,

3. To fpeak fincerely, I own it is my *private* opinion, that it has been too common a thing for people in New-England to exprefs themfelves in a manner juftly exceptionable upon thefe points, however agreeably both to the letter and fpirit of the articles aforefaid : But yet, I believe, not more exceptionably than many eminent divines of the Church of England did in the laft century.

4. It is probably true, that for half a century paft, many minifters and others in New-England have difcourfed more cautioufly upon thofe points than the greater part did before ; and fome perhaps have run into an oppofite extreme : Which may be owing to the prevalence of the church of England amongft us ; many of whofe minifters, if not the moft, have long preached in a ftrain almoft diametrically oppofite to the articles aforefaid. But upon fuppofition that we are really indebted to the Society or their miffionaries in any degree, for freeing the fpeculative doctrines of religion amongft us, from what Mr. *Apthorp* calls *fenfelefs horrors* ; (which will not be generally allowed) yet we may well think it ungenerous and inconfiftent in this gentleman, to revile

our

our Forefathers as a company of fuperſtitious, fenſeleſs Fanatics, for adhering ſo cloſely as they did to the doctrinal articles of the church of England.

Mr. *Apthorp* adds, as another particular of our reformation, which is greatly the work of the Society, that *hypocriſy has worn off in proportion as men have ſeen the beauty of holineſs.* As to which it may be obſerved, that we have not more clearly ſeen the *beauty of holineſs* ſince the prevalence of the church of England amongſt us, than it was diſcerned before, except perhaps by way of *contraſt.* He does not pretend to ſay, that the ſtate of religion has been improved here, ſince the miſſions, in reſpect of *morals, manners* or *piety.* So that the *holineſs* which he ſpeaks of, ſeems to be ſomething diſtinct from theſe ; and what ſort of holineſs that is, I will not pretend to conjecture. But whereas he ſuppoſes that *hypocriſy has worn off* in proportion to the glorious diſcovery of it in the church of England ; I muſt obſerve, that the moſt deteſtable hypocriſy in the ſight of God and wiſe men, is that which is ſhewn in a zeal for rites and ceremonies, for external modes and forms ; eſpecially uninſtituted ones, the inventions of men, while the zealots are comparatively negligent of the weightier matters of the law and goſpel. Of which kind of hypocriſy there has unqueſtionably been much more amongſt us, ſince the Society was inſtituted than before. But, to

what

what this is to be afcribed, is another queftion : I will not fay, it is *greatly the work of the Society.*

Mr. *Apthorp* fubjoins : *And above all, that exterminating monfter* perfecution, *is itfelf exterminated both from the temper and practice of the prefent age.* This he mentions as another inftance in which the ftate of religion is manifeftly improved among us, by means of the Society and the epifcopal miffions. And any one, ignorant of the country, would from hence naturally conclude, that there had been here *acts of uniformity* in worfhip, rigoroufly put in execution, till the eftablifhment of epifcopal churches in thefe parts : For otherwife this is not fo pertinently faid, as might be expected from fo ingenious a gentleman. But this is a miftake at beft : No fuch acts ever took place here, fo far as I have learnt. But if there were, in the early days of the country, fome inftances of unjuftifiable feverity towards the Quakers, &c. they were ufed much lefs under the notion of thefe people being diffenters from our mode of worfhip, than of their being difturbers of the peace, and of our religious affemblies ; in which refpects they were indeed very diforderly, abufive, and highly culpable. Some learned and good men in England, who had not a thorough underftanding of the cafe, have, for this reafon, paffed much too harfh a judgment on the conduct of our Forefathers ; tho' I will not undertake to vindicate all their conduct

relative

relative to this point. But suppoſing them to
have been juſtly chargeable with ſome inſtan-
ces of perſecution ; from whom ? — from
what church did they learn this practice ? E-
piſcopalians, certainly, ſhould lay their hands
upon their mouths—

Moreover : How blameable ſoever our
Forefathers might have been in this reſpect ;
yet how does it appear that our reformation
therein, is *greatly the work of the Society* ? Nothing of that kind had been known amongſt
us for many years before the Society had any
miſſionaries among us, or was itſelf in being.
Nor is it a little odd that this gentleman ſhould
inſinuate, that the poſterity of thoſe who ſo
cruelly perſecuted our Fathers out of England
into America, ſhould follow us hither to teach
us charity and moderation, and to extermi-
nate the *exterminating monſter perſecution* from
among us ! Is he in jeſt or in earneſt ? —
Wherever we learnt Chriſtian forbearance and
charity towards thoſe that differ from us, he
may be aſſured we did not learn it of the
church of England ; from which our beloved
and honoured brethren in England, even at
this day, do not in all reſpects find the kindeſt
uſage ; being ſubjected to divers temporal in-
conveniences on account of their non-conformity. And notwithſtanding the gentleman
ſays, perſecution is exterminated both from
the temper and practice of the preſent age ; I
have myſelf heard ſome of the epiſcopalians a-
mongſt

mongft us fpeak with much regret, and even indignation, of the *act of toleration*, by which that of *uniformity* was in part repealed. Nay, it is credibly reported, that fome of the warm epifcopalians here, have faid, *they hoped for the time when they might fhoot* diffenters *as freely as they might fhoot pigeons.* Not a few of them difcover a like fpirit. Let the reader then judge, whether the exterminating mon-fter is intirely exterminated ; and if fo, how *greatly this is the work of the Society* and their miffionaries.

It does not appear, upon the whole, that we are at all indebted to the Society for the improvement of the ftate of religion amongft us, in any of the inftances which this gentle-man mentions: It is probably in fome refpects, particularly as to our *morals*, worfe than if there had never been an epifcopal church in thefe parts. But upon fuppofition that what Mr. *Apthorp* fays as to this matter, was true in fact ; ftill it muft be remembered, that this is no juftification of the Society in alienating their fund and revenues from their direct, pro-per ends expreffed in the charter.

SECTION

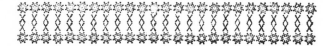

SECTION XIII.

*Farther Reflexions relative to the views
and Conduct of the Society, the State
of Religion in New-England, and the
prevalence of* Epifcopacy *here ; with
Remarks on fome expreffions in Dr.*
Bearcroft's *fermon before the Society,*
1744.

DR. BEARCROFT, who has many years
been Secretary to the Society, near the
beginning of his fermon before it, fpeaking of the defign of the inftitution, expreffes
himfelf in a very rhetorical ftile about the
great " charity of bringing back their brethren
" in America to good manners and a chriftian.
" life." And had he fpoken only of profeffed
epifcopalians, or of people in fuch an heathenifh ftate as thofe in fome of the colonies,
no one would have doubted the charitablenefs
of fuch a defign. But to me it is evident that
he comprehends us Congregationalifts and
Prefbyterians in New-England, in the terms
brethren in America. Taking this for granted,

it may be obferved, that how much foever we may be obliged to him for his catholicifm in acknowledging us for his brethren, notwith-ftanding our apoftacy from epifcopacy ; yet we are not much obliged to him for the infi-nuation, that we are fadly departed from good manners and a chriftian life ; fo that the de-fign of the Society *to bring us back* thereto, is produced as an argument of their prodigious charity. And if by thus bringing us back, he really intended any thing more than conver-ting us to epifcopacy ; the Society have hi-therto failed very much in their charitable de-fign. For though their miffionaries have, firft and laft, made a confiderable number of pro-felytes from our churches, many of whom needed to be bettered in their morals ; yet it may be queftioned whether any of them have thereby been brought back to good manners and a chriftian life : Poffibly there may have been fome, though I never knew an example of it. But the examples of the contrary are numerous : I mean, of perfons whofe morals, though not unexceptionable before, were ap-parently much worfe after their being thus epifcopally converted. It is a known fact a-mong us, that thefe profelytes often become exceeding loofe, profligate, vain and cenfori-ous ; feemingly placing no fmall part of their religion in railing at their *unconverted*, i. e. congregational and prefbyterian neighbours, whofe lives are chriftian, excepting this one

capital,

capital fault, that they go to MEETING every
Lord's-day !

THE Doctor a little afterwards feems to be
quite in a rapture, when he fays, " The word
" of God mightily grows and prevails in New
" England *according to the liturgy of the church*
" *of England.*" Brave indeed ! What good
news was this from a far country ?—that the
word of God fhould mightily prevail here *according to the liturgy* ; which he feems to confider as the ftandard, or the touchftone by
which *the word of God* was to be tried. I fuppofe he had lately been reading fome of the
pompous, hyperbolical accounts of the miffionaries concerning the fuccefs of their pious
labors. Of many of which accounts from
time to time, as to the number of their converts, baptifms, communicants, &c. I have at
prefent only time to fay, that no perfon who
knows any thing particularly about America,
can read them without aftonifhment ; tho' the
direct proof of a *negative* in fuch cafes, however falfe the accounts may be, is no eafy
matter—Could the Doctor have truly faid,
that pure religion mightily prevailed in New-
England according to the holy fcriptures, and
that the converts to the church were generally pious, virtuous and good men, it might
have been a triumph altogether as becoming
a Chriftian divine, as that the word of God
prevailed *according to the liturgy.* Or if he had
faid that the word, inventions and command-

N 2   ments

ments of men, mightily prevailed in New-
England *according to the liturgy*, he might perhaps have come nearer the truth. But with
fome gentlemen, it feems, the liturgy ! the liturgy ! is all and all. If that is embraced,
from whatever petulant, frivolous humour, or
difhonorable motive, O ! then to be fure the
word of God mightily grows and prevails; and
every *unftable* fon of REUBEN, every tho'tlefs,
giddy changeling or out-caft, is, without more
ado, reprefented as brought back to good
manners and a chriftian life. Thefe profelytes
are, perhaps, fpoken of in the accounts tranf-
mitted to the Society, as perfons of very good
characters, of much confideration ; and com-
mended for their penetration. I lately met
with a very remarkable account of the fagaci-
ty of fome of them in one of the *abftracts*, and
the prodigious improvement which they had
made in a fhort time under the documents of a
miffionary: It was to this purpofe ;--They had
difcovered that there were in the liturgy *no remains of popery* and the *mafs-book*, as they had
formerly fuppofed !———Nor are there a few
epifcopalians, who feem to have much the
fame opinion of *that compofition*, that the old
Ephefians had of their famous, adored image,
which, they were fo confident, *fell down immediately from Jupiter ;* and of their church,
that thofe zealots had of their goddefs, when
they bauled by the fpace of two hours together, *Great is Diana of the Ephefians !*

THE

THE Doctor says afterwards; "The powers
" there in being, [i. e. in New-England] to do
" them justice, had taken care for God's pub-
" lic worship, and erecting schools for the e-
" ducation of their youth "— What occasion
was there then for the Society to maintain
missions and schools here at a great expence,
to the neglect of the heathen, and of those
colonies in which no such pious care was taken by the government; which, according to
their charter, were the direct, proper objects
of their charity? Is not this at best very myste-
rious? O, no! the Doctor explains himself in
the next words — "but not in the true ortho-
" dox principles of the church of England."--
Sad indeed! And therefore we Congregati-
onalists and Presbyterians in New-England, being in so much worse a state than the others,
were proportionably so much the more proper
objects of the Society's charity; to the end that
the word of God might mightily grow and
prevail here *according to the liturgy;* whether
the heathen, and those that were but one degree better, had the word and gospel of God
preached to them at all or not—Here the Doctor explains at least the sentiments of his own
soul, probably the views of the Society also. But
can the unprejudiced even among the episcopalians, think it a matter of equal importance
to convert us to episcopacy, and some con-
fessedly *unnecessary* ceremonies, however *decent,*
as to propagate the knowledge of the only
true

trueGod and JefusChrift among the heathen, or in heathenifh places, where there is hardly any appearance of religion? It were doubtlefs better that WE fhould be deftitute of thofe supereminent, fuper-abundant, and, if I may be allowed the expreffion, fuper-fcriptural means of grace and falvation, which are to be had in the communion of the church of England, than that any of thofe for whom Chrift died, fhould perifh for want of God's *own word and facraments*, or be perverted to Popifh *fuperftition* and *idolatry*.

IT would doubtlefs rejoice the Doctor's heart, if *the powers here in being*, inftead of contenting themfelves with taking care for God's public worfhip according to his *own word* only, fhould be convinced of their error and neglect in this refpect ; and for the future take care for it *according to the liturgy* : Which may be about as much of an *improvement* upon the Bible, as fome of the Society's conduct is upon their original plan according to their charter. Yea, I believe it would not a little refrefh the good gentleman, only to hear that the *powers in being in New-England*, (if fuch a thing fhould ever be) on fome public occafion went in a body to church ; tho' it were only from the fame principle that the great *Syrian* Captain and Courtier formerly attended his royal mafter to the houfe of RIMMON, when he went to bow and worfhip there. § The Doctor might probably confider this as an indication,

§ 2 Kings Ch. VI.

dication, that they were gradually coming off
from their *ſtiſneſs* and *preciſeneſs* ; poſſibly
conclude, that in their hearts they condemned
their Forefathers ſeparation from the church
of England ; and intended to lead the riſing
generation into an opinion, that the differences betwixt that communion and ours are quite
inconſiderable.   How might this exalt his
hopes into a plerophory ?   And, that a ſure
preſage would it be, that the ges lious æra was
nigh at hand, when the word of GOD ſhould
ſtill more mightily grow and prevail in New-
England *according to the liturgy !* —

𝄢𝄢𝄢𝄢𝄢𝄢𝄢𝄢𝄢𝄢𝄢𝄢𝄢𝄢𝄢𝄢𝄢𝄢𝄢𝄢𝄢𝄢𝄢

SECTION XIV.

That the Society have long had a formal
deſign to root out Preſbyterianiſm *&c.*
and to eſtabliſhing both Epiſcopacy *and*
Biſhops *in the colonies : In purſuance*
of which favourite project, they have
in a great meaſure neglected the im-
portant ends of their inſtitution.

IT is hardly poſſible to account for the Society's conduct, without ſuppoſing them
to have had ſuch a deſign ; and this being
once ſuppoſed, it will ſerve to explain, and
ſhew

fhew the confiftency thereof ; not indeed
with the charter,but with itfelf. And as to the
truth of the faft, that they have long had this
defign; fuch evidence fhall now be produced,
as may *in this cafe* be deemed the beft, *their
own.*

IN the*Account of the Society*, publifhed 1706,
which has been mentioned before, after
fpeaking of ᴗ of " independent congregations "
in New-Englᵢᴄₒⱼ, they fay : " Several other
" ways of divifion and feparation did fo much
" obtain in other of our colonies and planta-
" tions, that this made it more neceffary to
" think of providing for a regular and ortho-
" dox miniftry to be fent and fettled amongft
" them ; to remove thofe *prejudices* under
" which the people generally laboured, *and*
" *to promote, as much as poffible,* anAGREEMENT
" *in faith and worfhip —*" † This can mean
nothing more or lefs than *uniformity*, or a
general *conformity* to the doctrine, difcipline
and worfhip of the church of England : Which
feems to have been what fome had in view,
even before the inftitution of theSociety; tho'
there is nothing in the charter which countenances the propagation of the church of England, in oppofition to other proteftant churches ; as before obferved.

IN the fame *Account* they fay, They have
been "careful of recommending the difcipline
" of the church of England, as far as the con-
" ftitution of thofe countries will *poffibly admit.*
" The

† *Account,* &c. p. 11.

" The want of a *Bishop* or suffragan in those
" parts was often complained of——And this
" matter has been carried as far as the difficulties
" in it would hitherto allow, and is under such
" farther solicitation and advances, that we hope
" *shortly* to see a happy success of it. In the
" mean time, all young students in those parts,
" who desire *episcopal* ordination, are invited in-
" to England; and their *expences* in coming and
" returning are to be *defrayed* by the Society."†

In the *Abstract* printed 1711, they say, " It
" having been frequently represented to the So-
" ciety, that there is great want of a Bishop to
" govern those missionaries, whom the Society
" has or shall, from time to time, send over to
" New-England,—as well as the rest of the
" clergy in those and the adjacent colonies; and
" to ordain others, and to confirm the children
" of the clergy and laity; this matter has been
" most seriously considered of, and is yet de-
" pending before the Society, and in the mean
" time, and *till they can bring it to bear*, they
" are looking out for the best and most commo-
" dious place,—to fix the *See* for the said Bi-
" shop."—‡

Dr. KENNET, a member of the Society,
part of whose letter to Dr. COLMAN was quoted before, says in another paragraph, " It is our
" being *misinformed* and *misguided* in some ways,
" that increases our desires of having *Bishops*
" settled in those foreign parts committed to
" our care—I hope *your churches* would not
" be *jealous* of it," &c.

O   IN

† P. 74.   ‡ *Abstract* 1711. p. 27, 28.

In the *Abstract* printed 1715, the Society
say, "After all, upon the renewed instances
"from the *governors of provinces*, ministers,
"vestries, and private persons in the plantations,
"for settling ecclesiastical *Superiors* there, with-
"out whom the *church must rather decrease*
"*than increase;* and from a full conviction of
"the expediency thereof, *Bishops* being never
"more wanted there than now; the Society's
"endeavours have been employed, not without
"*expence* this year, in *paving the way for such,*
"by all proper *applications*, and due *prepara-*
"*tions:* Not to mention what has been for-
"merly done in this matter," † &c.—And by
"way of preparation for a *Suffragan*, or *Bishop*,
"in one of the *Sees* upon the continent of
"America; the Society having thought fit to
"purchase a seat for his residence some while
"since at 600 l. sterling expence," ‡ &c. There
are several pages of this *Abstract* fill'd with this
affair of *Bishops* in America. Later *Abstracts*
and other records might easily be produced, in
order to shew what a favourite object this has
been with the Society. And one standing instruction of the Society to their missionaries, is
in these remarkable words, *viz.* "X. That they
"*frequently* visit their respective parishioners;
"those of *our own communion*, to keep them stea-
"dy in the profession and practice of religion,
"as taught in the church of England; and those
"that *oppose us*, or *dissent from us*, to CONVINCE
"and RECLAIM them," &c. This clearly shews
what they are after. It will also be observed
here,

† P. 52. ‡ P. 54.

here, that WE are confidered as PARISHIONERS
of the miffionaries, no lefs than profeffed epifcopalians: And we are often fpoken of AS SUCH
by them in their letters to the Society, as appears by the *Abftracts*. How *affuming* is this!——

THE affair of Bifhops has lately been, and probably now is in agitation in England. And we
fee the Society fpare neither *endeavours, applications,* nor *expence,* in order to effect their grand
defign of *epifcopizing* (if I may ufe the term)
all New-England, as well as the other colonies.
And it is fuppofed by many, that a certain *fuperb
edifice* in a neighbouring town, was even from
the foundation defigned for the *Palace* of one
of the *humble fucceffors* of the apoftles.

BUT however that matter may be, the following things are evident:

1. THAT the Society have long had a formal
defign to diffolve and root out all our New-
England churches; or, in other words, to re-
duce them all to the epifcopal form; or, in the
words of their *own Account,* before cited, " to
" promote, *as much as poffible* an *agreement*
" [uniformity] in faith and worfhip"——

2. THIS fully and clearly accounts for their
being fo ready to encourage *fmall epifcopal parties* all over New-England, by fending them
miffionaries, &c. altho' the people had the
" means of religion already, in other proteftant
" communions." For thefe handfuls of people,
fcattered here and there, it is fuppofed, or at
leaft hoped, will in time, by fome means or
other, become confiderable for numbers; and
at length eat out, or abforb all our churches.

O 2   BUT

BUT ſuppoſing them finally to carry this favourite point, at a vaſt expence, as I hope in God they never will; yet one would think it impoſſible even for themſelves to imagine, that the intereſt of religion in the colonies would be a quarter part ſo much ſerved hereby, as if they had employed this money in thoſe ways which are plainly pointed out in the charter, and from which they have alienated it. Is the effecting an exact *uniformity* among us in diſcipline, modes of worſhip, ceremonies, &c. an object worthy of any attention or expence, in compariſon with that of maintaining a public worſhip in places deſtitute thereof, or the converſion of the heathen! Can wiſe men, free from bigotry and the ſpirit of party, poſſibly think it is, tho' they are themſelves epiſcopalians in ſentiment?

SECTION XV.

That by ſupporting little Epiſcopal Parties in New-England, and endeavouring to convert Presbyterians, &c. to the Church of England, contrary to the whole ſpirit of the Charter, the Society have actually defrauded the People who were the proper Objects of their Charity.

IF the Society's fund, together with the annual collections, legacies, &c. had been more than adequate to the real exigencies

of

of thofe people, who were indifputably the proper objects of that charitable inftitution ; and they had applied only the *furplufage* for the fupport and encouragement of the epifcopal party in New-England, in oppofition to prefbyterians, &c. their conduct would have been much lefs exceptionable than it is: Since, upon this fuppofition, others would not have been *injured* by fuch an application. Tho' even in this cafe, it might well be queftioned whether their conduct would have been entirely juftifiable ; becaufe their charter warrants neither their receiving nor expending any money for fupporting any one party whatfoever amongft proteftants, in oppofition to another; but only for the common caufe of *Chriftianity,* in oppofition to atheifm, infidelity and popery.   But the Society have by no means thus abounded in money. They have been making great complaints for half a century paft, how ftreightened they were for money ; how much their annual expences exceeded their certain annual income.   Dr. HUTTON, bifhop of Bangor, in his fermon before the Society 1745, (p. 24.) fays, they have borne " an expence frequently more than *five* " *times* equal to their certain annual income." Thefe reprefentations have been very pathetically made from time to time, in order to induce good people of *all denominations* to affift them in fo pious a work, as that of fupporting the public worfhip of God in thofe colonies which muft otherwife be deftitute of it, and propagating the gofpel among the poor *Negroes* and
Indians.

Indians. This ſhall at any time be proved at large by quotations from the ſermons, and other publications of the Society, if any perſon of reputation denies it, as I am confident no one will preſume to do. And yet, while theſe loud, and almoſt tragical complaints have been making, the Society have been expending large ſums every year in New-England, quite beyond the deſign of their inſtitution, to ſupport and increaſe the epiſcopal party as ſuch; greatly to the neglect of the Southern colonies upon the continent, the Indians bordering upon us, the Weſt India iſlands, and the many thouſands of Negro ſlaves in them; all of which and whom were the direct proper objects of their charity; and whoſe *names* were made uſe of moſt pathetically, to excite compaſſion in, and draw money from well diſpoſed people of *every* denomination! It needs no proof, that by how much more was done by the Society for the ſupport of the epiſcopal party here; by ſo much leſs muſt unavoidably have been done for the heathen, or for the colonies in a ſtate but little better than that of heatheniſm. And if the Society cannot, in this reſpect, be ſaid to have " robbed-other churches," to eaſe and gratify the epiſcopalians here; yet they may be ſaid to have *robbed* the heathen, the ſlaves, and heatheniſh colonies aforeſaid; who had an excluſive right, according to the charter, to the benefit of that very money which has been ſunk in the epiſcopal gulph here, where the people actually " had the means of religion in other proteſtant communions."

munions." He that can confider thefe facts, and fuch a flagrant abufe of a noble inftitution, without *admiration*, has doubtlefs that qualification which the poet fpeaks of, as the moft effential foundation of happinefs—

Nil admirari prope res eft una, Numici,
Solaq; quæ poffit facere & fervare beatum.

EVEN upon fuppofition that the Society has fuch an extraordinary " difcretionary power" as Mr. *Apthorp* fpeaks of; (which will hereafter be confidered) fo that they cannot be juftly charged with violating their charter, by expending their money for the fupport of an epifcopal party in New-England, to the prejudice of other colonies, &c. or if they have a *legal right* to act thus; yet in how extraordinary and unaccountable a manner do they ufe that fuppofed right and power? Can any wife and candid man, who allows the main facts and circumftances as before reprefented, poffibly think the interefts of CHRIST's kingdom fo much ferved in this way, as they might have been by a different conduct in the Society? If they are not, this is certainly a mifapplication both of their charity and their power, in fome degree. For whatever powers or monies the Society are entrufted with, they were to be employed in fuch a manner as fhould moft effectually anfwer the ends exprefly mentioned in their charter. And they have all along profeffed to apply their fund and revenues in fuch a manner as fhould be likely to do the moft good, and beft to ferve the general intereft of religion in the colonies, and adja-
ccnt

eent countries. That they have not done fo,
but alienated their revenues from a truly noble
to a comparatively mean, narrow, party defign,
is as certain as any thing of this nature can
be: Tho' I would by no means be underftood as
charging fo refpectable a Body with any wilful,
criminal abufe of power, or mifapplication of
monies.

****

SECTION XVI.

*Of the good that might probably have been
done, had the Monies which have been
mifapplied in fupporting the* Epifcopal
Party *in* New-England, *been applied according to the true and noble Defign
of the Inftitution.*

IT is no inconfiderable fum that the Society
have funk in the epifcopal gulph here in
New-England, quite beyond, and therefore
contrary to, the defign of their inftitution; there
being no medium, as has before been obferved,
betwixt a right application of their fund, conformable to their charter, and a perverfion of
it. According to the *Abftract* 1730, £. 705
fterling was expended on the miffions, &c. in
New-England. In 1739, the fum was £. 1030
fterling. And in 1761, the lateft *Abftract* which
I have been able to procure, it was £. 1270.
Thefe

These disbursements, it must be remembered, are exclusive of books to be distributed, and other incidental charges. So that, according to a moderate calculation, there may have been about £.1200 sterling expended by the Society for N. England, one year with another, for 32 years past; amounting to   38,400
And about £.200 per *Annum* for 20
years preceeding 1730,amounting to   4,000
                                      ————
Total   Er. excepted,   42,400 sterl.

BUT then a deduction is to be made on account of that part of this sum which may have been expended conformably to the design of the charter, in supporting the public worship in some places in N. England, particularly Rhode-Island government, where the Society's charity was needed. If we deduct £.7400, there has been about 35,000 sterl. misapplied in N. England,according to the reasoning in the preceeding sections. I shall take the liberty to go upon this supposition, tho' I do not pretend to be very exact as to the *quantum*; I believe it is not less than that. The benefit of this sum then, other persons, the Negro slaves, Indians and heathenish colonies, have been deprived of; tho' the money was as it were collected in *their name*, or with a profession of employing it in *their* service.

Now let it be considered, how much good might probably have been done to the souls of these people, the direct, proper objects of this charity, had the aforesaid sum of 35,000 sterl.

P   been

been duly applied in maintaining and propagating chriſtianity among them, inſtead of being laid out to ſupport and increaſe the epiſcopal party in thoſe towns of N. England, in which people " had the means of religion already, in " *other proteſtant communions.*" Forty or fifty miſſions might, with this ſum, have been comfortably maintained among the heathen, and in heatheniſh places, every year, for more than thirty years paſt ; and a conſiderable number for ſeveral years antecedent thereto. It is well known that in ſome of the Southern colonies, there are large diſtricts of 10, 20, 30, and 40 miles extent, and I think more, wherein there is no publick worſhip of any kind regularly kept up, for want of miniſters; in which colonies there are alſo many Roman-catholics and ſlaves. And their ſtate, to this day, anſwers very exactly to the deſcription in the charter, of thoſe places which are therein marked out as the objects of this charitable inſtitution. The ſame in general is applicable to ſome of our Weſt-India iſlands, all which ſo much abound with Negro ſlaves.

LET us ſuppoſe then, that about one half the aforeſaid ſum had been employed in ſupporting miſſions and ſchools in thoſe colonies, and the other half among the *Indians* bordering upon us. How much good might probably have been done, by keeping up ſome form of religion, and giving a *check* at leaſt to infidelity, vice and barbarity in the former ; and by propagating the knowledge of true religion amongſt the latter .

In

In what degree it might have pleafed almighty God to fucceed thefe miffions, it is indeed impoffible for man particularly to fay. But fuch an application of the money would unqueftionably have been right and proper, according to the charter : And the defign had at leaft been charitable, noble and laudable, whatever the fuccefs had been. Nor is there any reafon to doubt in general, but that fome, yea, great good would have been done, if all the mifapplied money had been difcretely expended in thefe ways. The general ftate of religion in thofe colonies would, in all probability, have been much better at this day than it is. Many perfons might have been reftrained from open vice and impiety ; not a few brought to a ferious fenfe and practice of religion ; a great number of the Negro flaves in, and the Indians near the colonies, brought to fome hopeful knowledge of God and his truth had as many pious, and duly qualified miffionaries been fent to one and the other, for thirty or forty years paft, as might have been tolerably fubfifted on the aforefaid fum, which has been very little, if any thing better than thrown away ; yea, which many think really worfe than thrown away, all circumftances confidered. Nor am I either afhamed or afraid to own myfelf of this latter opinion ; being perfuaded that there is lefs real religion now in thofe parts of N. England where it has been expended, than there would have been, had it been funk in the ocean inftead of the epifcopal gulph here : Tho' it is

P 2

not

not to be fuppofed that any epifcopalians can be of this opinion ; neither is any ftrefs laid upon it in the prefent argument. But even allowing that fome good has been done by converting a number of prefbyterians, &c. to the church of England ; yet what fober and candid perfon can poffibly imagine, that the common caufe of chriftianity has been a tenth part fo much ferved hereby, as might have been reafonably expected from a different application of this money, in ways directly and indifputably agreeable to the intent of the charter ? What the venerable So-ciety may think of thefe things, I cannot pre-tend to fay : But I know, many wife and good men think they have reafon to blefs God, that they are not themfelves to give an account to him for fuch managements ; and that the blood of fo many as have probably perifhed thereby, *will not be required at* THEIR *hands.*

SECTION XVII.

Farther Reflections on the Society*s neglect-ing the Southern* Colonies *and the* Indians; *and a particular Inftance of the latter, with Refpect to the* Iroquois, *or* Five (*alias* Six) Nations.

THO' I will not affirm it for truth, yet I have been very credibly informed that the

people

people in some of the Southern colonies, and particularly in those parts of N. Carolina which were intirely destitute of ministers, have made earnest and repeated applications to the Society for missionaries to be sent to *them* ; sometimes without any answer at all, for years together ; and at last without success. And some solid, sensible and serious persons from that country, with whom I conversed in Boston several years ago, I think gave me the same account : But whether they did or not, I know they made such a representation of their sad state for want of ministers, and expressed so serious a desire of having the public worship of God introduced among them, that at this very moment it is not in my power to refrain from tears in reflecting on it—What they told me, at least confirms in some measure the report aforesaid, concerning the ineffectual sollicitations from thence to the Society ; who perhaps had it not in their power to comply therewith, by reason of the large expence which they were at in the noble design of supporting and increasing little episcopal parties, or factions, here and there in N. England. And according to the *Abstract*, 1761, the Society had only five missionaries in the whole country of N. Carolina, while they had about thirty in N. England ; chiefly in the most populous towns of it, where a due and legal provision was made for the support of ministers, and the public worship of God !

As to the Indians ; no one can doubt but that there have been, and still are, some great discou-

ragements

ragements in attempting to chriftianize them. But, according to divers appearances, the Society have had this work lefs at heart than that of propagating the peculiarities of epifcopacy and the liturgy in N. England, in oppofition to prefbyterianifm and congregationalifm. The neglect of the Natives in America, has long been complained of, and the accufation in fome fort allowed to be juft by themfelves, in times paft. This will appear in part from Bp. WILLIAMS's fermon before the Society, 1705. " But whilft we find *fault* " with others," fays he, " we muft not forget " *our own*. It has been the continual matter of " *reproach* to us, that this application to the " *Natives* has been *neglected on our part*. Where " are the numbers you have converted to the " Chriftian faith ? Where the fruits of your re- " ligion ? when you have under your care thofe " vaft dominions which are called the *Englifh* " *empire* ; and from whence you draw fo much " of your emoluments to enrich and pleafure " yourfelves at home. This is an objection that " *has its weight*, and perhaps is *uncapable* of a " juft and fufficient anfwer. Recriminations are " but a kind of confeffion of guilt : And the " beft way to anfwer, is, *to mend what is amifs* " *in ourfelves*"———*.

IT is unneceffary to confirm and juftify this complaint by an appeal to any of the later fermons before the Society ; which would be no difficult matter. Some effays they have indeed made

* 1 Edit. p. 32.

made from time to time, towards the converfion of the Savages : but they feem to have been very faint and feeble ; and with a fparing hand as to money, when compared with the goodnefs and importance of the work, or the difficulties to be expected in it ; with the zeal of our French neighbours to chriftianize, or rather *popize* the Indians, and even with their *own zeal* and expences in order to *epifcopize* the Congregationalifts and Prefbyterians of N. England. I am not ignorant however, that they and their miffionaries have frequently given the world fufficiently pompous accounts of their efforts in order to the converfion of the Indians ; not to fay, fpoken fomewhat hyperbolically of the real and great difficulties attending this work. Tho' I doubt not but that the Society kept to the accounts given them by their miffionaries ; who feem to have been lefs indefatigable, and fooner difcouraged in their labors among the Indians than among Us. And tho' the following remark of Dr. DOUGLASS, a very attentive and capable obferver of what paffed in the colonies, is not literally true of *all* the miffionaries in America, yet it deferves notice here : " The miffionaries from " the Society," fays he, " do not *in the leaft* " attempt the converfion of the Indians, *becaufe* " *it requires travel, labor and hardfhip.*" ‡

IT is certain from authentic records, even from feveral publications of the Society, that the *Five*, alias *Six nations*, a refpectable and war-like

people

‡ *Summary Hiftorical and Political, &c.* Vol. II. p. 118.

people on the Frontiers of N. York and Penn-
fylvania, and long the terror of all the other
Indians from Florida to the n. weſt of Canada,
have not only been our good friends and allies
all along, but for more than half a century paſt,
very favourably difpofed towards Chriſtianity ;
at leaſt towards entertaining miſſionaries among
them, which was a very important point gained.
Their chiefs have even petitioned for them re-
peatedly ; of which the Society was duly adver-
tiſed by the Governor of N. York, as appears
from the *Abſtracts*,&c. Nor have they been *wholly*
neglected by the Society ; than which, it is apprehended, little more can be ſaid, notwithſtanding all that Mr. *Apthorp* has written concerning
their " unwearied zeal in this attempt †". In
ſpeaking of this matter, Mr. *Apthorp* has referred
to Dr. BARCLAY, now a miſſionary in the city
of N. York ; who was for a time a miſſionary
to theſe Indians. It will not therefore be improper to obſerve a few things relative to that
worthy gentleman's miſſion to the *Iroquois*, or
Six Nations aforeſaid, as a ſpecimen of the Society's zeal for the converſion of the Indians *.

IN the year 1738 Mr. SERGEANT, the then
very worthy miſſionary to a tribe of Indians on
our weſtern frontiers, employed by the Boſton-
commiſſioners of the *Society for the propagation of*
                                                            the

---

† *Conſid.* p. 15, 16.
* The following facts relative to Mr. now Dr. *Barclay's* Indian
miſſion, are taken from the *Hiſtorical Memoirs* relating to the
Houſatonnuk Indians, and the excellent Mr. *Sergeant*, a Miſſionary to the latter from *another Society* : By the Rev. S. *Hopkins*, A. M. a gentleman of undoubted veracity, Page 66, &c.

the gospel in N. England, *and the parts adjacent in America,* incorporated Anno 1661 ; a (Society which pursues the true end of its institution) wrote the following letter to the Hon. and Rev. commissioners his employers, relative to Mr. BARCLAY and his mission.—" I had just now a letter," says he, " from Mr. BARCLAY, a young " gentleman of Albany, lately arriv'd from " London with a mission from the *Society for* " *the propagation of the Gospel in foreign parts,* " to the *Mohawks* * West of Albany ; who tells " me he has but a *scanty allowance,* (i. e. *from* " *the Society*) and could obtain NO *salary for an* " *interpreter,* or *school-master :* and that he has " thoughts of applying to the *commissioners at* " *Boston* for assistance ; but would have my ad- " vice first. I cannot tell what stock the corpo- " ration has ; but I suppose it is scanty, by the " allowances they afford their missionaries. How- " ever, I could heartily recommend Mr. BAR- " CLAY to the notice and favor of the *commissi-* " *oners.* He is a worthy gentleman, and well " deserves encouragement in his undertaking,"&c.

THE Rev. Mr. HOPKINS, after quoting this letter in his *Memoirs,* says : " That the reader " may be sensible what a prospect there was of " Mr. BARCLAY's being eminently serviceable " among the *Mohawks,* if he had been *duly en-* " *couraged ;* I shall (asking Mr. BARCLAY's " pardon) show by transcribing some passages

Q " contained

* N. B. The *Mohawks* are a principal Tribe of the *Iroquois,* or *Six Nations.*

" contained in his letter to Mr. SERGEANT.
" The following are from a letter wrote before
" he went for *orders*, and dated in his school at
" *Fort-Hunter*, June 11, 1736." The quotations ſtand thus in the *Memoirs* aforeſaid.

" I am heartily glad to hear of your ſucceſs ;
" I pray God more abundantly to bleſs and ſuc-
" ceed your labors : and may you enjoy abun-
" dant ſatisfaction in the diſcharge of your func-
" tion here, and a glorious reward hereafter. I
" bleſs God I have *no reaſon* to deſpair of ſuc-
" ceſs in my miſſion. They daily become more
" and more deſirous of inſtruction ; and would,
" in all probability, make great progreſs both in
" the knowledge and practice of Chriſtianity,
" were proper methods taken to inſtruct them.
" But I labor under *great diſadvantage for want*
" *of an interpreter* ; ſo that I cannot tell what
" progreſs they may make in knowledge, nor
" can I proceed regularly in my inſtructions ;
" and I muſt deſpair of obtaining a perfect know-
" ledge of their language, without the aſſiſtance
" of an interpreter, which could I but enjoy *for*
" *the ſpace of two or three years*, I doubt not
" but that I ſhould be maſter of it ; and ſhould
" take greater pleaſure and ſatisfaction in the diſ-
" charge of my duty. Nevertheleſs I have the
" comfort of ſeeing a *very great and daily re-*
" *formation of manners among them*, which is in-
" deed the end of all our endeavours——— I am
" almoſt amazed at the progreſs the youth make
" in reading and writing their own language.
                                          " All

" All the young men from 20 to 30 years, con-
" ftantly attend fchool when at home, and *will*
" *leave a frolic räther than mifs.* Sundry of
" them write as good a hand as myfelf (*which*
" *was very fair and good*)——As to the *encou-*
" *ragement* I have, for aught I fee yet, I muft
" expect my reward in another world. I have
" now been here almoft a year and half, but
" have never received a farthing from any body.
" The *Affembly* voted me *thirty pounds* for two
" years ; but by reafon of——I am not like to
" get it 'till a Governor comes over ; and have
" no great hope of farther encouragement from
" them." [N. B. This relates to the government of N. York.]

" As for the *Society*, they have allowed me
" *thirty pounds* for one year : What further
" encouragement they will give me, I know not.
" In the mean time I am at great charges. My
" board is *fix fhillings* a week, which is not a-
" bove half my neceffary expence."

MORE than two years after Mr. BARCLAY
had taken *Orders*, he wrote thus in another letter dated at Albany *Aug.* 21, 1740. " I am fa-
" tisfied I fhould have much greater fuccefs, if I
" had a *fchool-mafter* and *interpreter.* I had the
" fatisfaction laftLord's day to preach to a num-
" ber of the *Six Nations*, who came to this
" town to treat with the Governor, who alfo
" was prefent ; and has taken a great deal of
" pains to countenance my defign. My *Mohawk*
" congregation behav'd fo well, that all the au-

Q 2   ditory

" ditory were exceedingly delighted. I affure
" you I have the caufe at heart, and am well
" perfuaded of your zeal."—

From the foregoing reprefentation it is evident, that a wide door was opened for the gofpel
to enter among thofe heathen tribes : The fields
were white unto the harveft, had but labourers
been fent, and duly encouraged to the noble
work. Thefe tribes would probably have been
in general profeffed Chriftians before this day,
had the bufinefs been duly forwarded and encouraged. Which might perhaps, by reafon of the
great fame of the *Iroquois*, have had a very extenfive and happy influence on many other nations. But, alas ! the Society, tho' fo defirous
of chriftianizing the natives, could not afford
falaries to a fchool-mafter and interpreter, of perhaps about £.20 or £.30 fterling each ; nor to
Mr. Barclay himfelf, who was fo zealous in
this good caufe, half a proper fupport ! Why
not ? The reafon was apparently this ; that they
fupported fo many miffionaries here in N.. England at a great expence, for the encouragement
of the epifcopal party, and in order to convert
us to the liturgy. If fo great a proportion of
their revenue had not been thus unprofitably
funk in places where God's word and facraments
were duly adminiftred, how eafy would it have
been for them to fupport 5, 6, or more miffionaries, and as many interpreters and fchool-mafters
among the *Iroquois* ? Mr. *Apthorp* fpeaking of the
" promifing appearance" there was among the
                                                Iroquois

Iroquois about this time, fays, " — From the
" lateft authorities — we find this miffion either
" much dwindled, or greatly interrupted."†—
No wonder, when the miffion itfelf was fo ftar-
ved.   The Indians doubtlefs perceived how re-
mifs the Englifh were in the caufe, fo that they
could hardly think them in earneft ; and the
French jefuits, or other emiffaries, no queftion
made their advantage of this negligence.   Can it
be expected that miffions will fucceed, which are
conducted after fuch a manner ?—This fpecimen
may perhaps ferve to explain and confirm what
Mr. *Apthorp* fays, where he introduces the affair
the *Mohawks* ; — " *Indian* converfions are un-
" dertaken by *our* Society *incidentally,* and as it
" were *ex abundanti* ‡ ".   They have indeed been
undertaken—*as it were ;* but the words *ex abundanti,* methinks, found but odly here.   And to
reconcile what he immediately fubjoins, with
plain facts, even with relation to this very miffion
which he fo much glories in, is impoffible———
" Yet," fays he, " have they *omitted no opportu-
" nity* of promoting this pious work, *as far as
" they found it practicable.* *

† *Confid* p 16.   ‡ p. 15.

* N. B. There have lately been two miffionaries fent to the *Six
Nations* from Bofton, at the expence of the *other London Society,*
and the *Society in Scotland for propagating Chriftian knowledge.*
And the accounts received from them, as to the temper and dif-
pofition in which they find the Indians, are very encouraging, notwithftanding all the pretences, that it is a vain thing to attempt
the chriftianizing of *Savages.*   If there had been as much zeal
for converting them to Chrift, as there has been for converting
Us to epifcopacy, the real obftacles in the way of it would have
doubtlefs appeared lefs formidable than they have been reprefented.

SECTION XVIII.

Of the important political ends *that might have been anfwered, had the Society taken due care to fend proper Miffionaries to the* Indians ; *and the pernicious Confequences of their Neglect.*

THE author of thefe obfervations is fenfible that worldly politics, and temporal things were not the direct objects of this inftitution ; but the promotion of true religion, and the eternal happinefs of men. However, thefe things often ftand in a clofe connexion, and are in a meafure interwoven with each other. And the Society's profecuting that important part of their plan, the converfion of the heathen bordering on our American colonies, would at the fame time have anfwered very valuable ends of a political nature. This, one would think, was an *additional* obligation lying upon them to do fo, inftead of neglecting it for the fake of converting us to the liturgy, in the manner they have done. That fuch ends would, in all probability, have been anfwered thereby ; and that this neglect has been attended with very fatal confequences in a civil confideration of things, may appear from the following remarks.

IT is known that the Indian nations lie on the back of our fettlements, from N. Scotia Northward,

Northward, round to the Weft and S. Weft as far as Georgia and Florida. And had early and due care been taken by theSociety to fend as many miffionaries among them, as could have been fubfifted on the money fo unprofitably funk in N. England ; it would have had a direct and manifeft tendency to attach them to the Britifh intereft. Had this £.35,000 fterl. or the greater part of it, been employed in maintaining a number of fenfible, difcrete minifters among the Indians, and enabling them to make them fmall prefents from time to time, in order to gain their efteem and good-will, it might probably have been the means, not only of giving them at leaft fome favourable impreffions of Chrifti-anity in general, but of the proteftant religion ; and fo making the greater part of them our faft friends.

And there was the more occafion for taking this courfe, in order to counter-act the defigns of the French, till of late our dangerous ene-mies and rivals on this continent. They, if not from a principle of piety, yet of found policy, have all along made a point of fending jefuits, priefts and other emiffaries to all the Indian tribes that would admit them. It is evident that the Society were not ignorant of thefe circumftances; which were well known to the Britifh court, even before the charter was granted ; and in all pro-bability, were one reafon of its being granted. It may be added, that the Society did, from the firft, *profefs* to have a regard to them. The

following

following extracts from the *Account of the Society*,
will ferve at once to throw light upon this affair,
and to render their neglect the more *unaccounta-*
ble. They fay, ' Nor hath the Society been
• unmindful of ufing their *utmoft endeavours* for
' propagating the gofpel among the heathen *In-*
• *dians* and flaves in and near our plantations.
' They received with great fatisfaction a letter
' from the *Lords commiffioners of trade and plan-*
• *tations,* directed to the Ld. arch. bp. of Canter-
' bury, fignifying, " That the earl of Bellamont
" had feveral times reprefented to them the great
" want of fome minifters of the church of
" England, to inftruct the Five Nations of In-
" dians on the frontiers of N. York, and *pre-*
" *vent their being practis'd upon by French priefts*
" *and jefuifts."*— ' At the fame time the Lords
' commiffioners imparted to his Grace, and to
' the Lord bp. of London, fome farther advice
' upon the fubject—in particular this remarkable
' extract of what was faid by One in the name
' of the reft of the *Sachems*—to the commiffio-
' ners for the Indian affairs in Albany, June 28,
' 1706—Says he, " We are now come to trade ;
" and not to fpeak of religion.   Only thus much
" I muft fay, all the while I was here, before I
" went to Canada, I never heard any thing
" talk'd of religion, or the leaft mention made
" of converting us to the Chriftian faith.   And
" we fhall be *glad* to hear, if at laft you are fo
" pioufly inclined to take pains to inftruct your
" Indians in the Chriftian religion.   I will not
say

" fay but that it may induce fome to return to
" their native country. *I wifh it had been done*
" *fooner*, that you had had minifters to inftruct
" your Indians in the Chriftian faith," &c.
' This reprefentation,' the Society add, ' was laid
' before the Queen in council ; from whence
' his Grace the Archbifhop of Canterbury re-
' ported this order.

At the Court at St. James's, &c.

" Upon reading this day at the Board a re-
" prefentation——fetting forth, among other
" things, that as to the Five Nations bordering
" on New-York, left the intrigues of the French
" in Canada, and the influence of their priefts,
" who frequent and converfe, and fometimes in-
" habit with thofe Indians, fhould debauch them
" from her Majefty's allegiance, their Lordfhips
" are humbly of opinion—that two proteftant
" minifters be appointed," &c. The Society add,
' Upon communicating this order to the Society,
' it was immediately agreed, that it fhould be
' referred to a committee,' &c. †

THE chief defign of this quotation, is to fhew
how early and fully the Society were apprifed
of the intrigues of the French with the Indians
on this continent, and the importance of counter-acting their defigns, in a political as well as
religious confideration of things. Thefe things
they have known all along, from the very foundation of the Society. And yet, that they have
done hardly any thing towards the converfion
of the Indians; and either could not or would

R   not

† *Account, &c.* p. 38...41. printed 1706.

not allow even an interpreter or School-mafter
to Mr. BARCLAY, is equally certain: Their
object, to all appearance, having been rather the
extirpation of prefbyterianifm and congregation-
ifm from the colonies, than the planting of
Chriftanity among the Indians; whereby they
might at once have been inftrumental of faving
many fouls, and doing an important fervice to
Great-Britain.

HAD the Society applied the money which
they have funk in New-England, (in a way
quite unauthorized by their charter) to the fupport of miffions among the Indians, it is quite
probable, as was intimated before, that the greater part of thofe bordering on our colonies might
long fince have received very favourable impreffions of the Chriftian, proteftant religion,
and been amicable to us. We fhould of courfe
have had a much larger fhare of the profitable trade with them, which has been almoft
engroffed by the French. And, as many of
them might have been in a degree civilized at
the fame time, and brought into the Englifh
way of living; they would of courfe have
taken off a greater quantity of Britifh manu-
factures, and other commodities, to the national
advantage. The lives of great numbers of Britifh fubjects in the plantations, deftroyed by the
Savages from time to time, would have been
faved. The colonies which have been kept
in terror, and ftunted in their growth, their
frontiers having often been quite cut off, or
broken up, would have been in a much more
flourifhing

flourishing condition than they are at present. And most of these Indians, instead of being at the command of the French, to cut our throats and scalp us, whenever they thought proper ; might have been ready to act for us against them, on any just occasion.

THESE are some of the important political ends that might probably have been answered, had the Society thought proper to send missionaries among the Indians, (whose conversion they have all along declared to be a principal, tho' not a primary object with them) instead of sinking so much money in the episcopal gulph in New-England. And when we also consider how duly they have been advertised of the French intrigues from time to time, and of the importance of counter-acting them ; it is not easy to say, whether their piety or their patriotism is the most conspicuous, with relation to this part of their conduct. And, whether their affection for, and strong attachment to the peculiarities of a *party*, are not at least as conspicuous as either of them, the reader who is not afraid to think, is left to judge from the whole series of facts and circumstances.

SECTION XIX.

SECTION XIX.

Of the discretionary Power *of the Society,
and Mr. Apthorp's Reasoning thereon.*

THE ingenious Mr. *Apthorp*, to whom I
must now again pay my devoirs, urges
the large discretionary power of the Society, in order to vindicate their conduct. The
passage to which I refer, seems to have something so very *curious* in it, that I cannot but
quote it at large for the *entertainment* of the
reader.

" It is observable," says he, " that a *large*
" *discretionary power* is left to the Society, to
" regulate their institution, *and even occasionally*
" *to make* ALTERATIONS in it, in such a man-
" ner as to render it most beneficial to religion,
" whether in our colonies, or among the bor-
" dering nations. For this purpose, they and
" their successors for ever are empowered to
" make any laws or constitutions that shall seem
" reasonable, profitable or requisite for the good
" estate and government of the Society, and the
" effectual promoting its *charitable design.*
" Thus, *with an evidence beyond exception,* it
" appears that their conduct in placing churches
" AMONG US, *is in all respects* CONFORMABLE
" *to their institution*"——†

1. IT

1. IT is to be obferved, that Mr. *Apthorp* here refers to that part of the charter which relates to by-laws; but in quoting which (p. 10.) he has tranfpofed fome claufes and omitted others, without giving notice of it to his readers in the ufual way. However, fince in his own way of quoting it, there does not feem to be any very material alteration in the fenfe; it will not be worth while to compare the quotation and charter together, merely for the fake of fhewing fome of his harmlefs errors. But had a reputed Scholar quoted any difputed paffage in LIVY, TACITUS or CICERO, in the manner in which this gentleman quoted another part of the charter, before taken notice of; it would have been no eafy matter for him ever to regain his reputation in the learned world. Whether mifquoting the charter in this controverfy, is not an offence of a much higher nature, is fubmitted to the judgment of the impartial reader.

2. IT feems a pretty extraordinary pofition, that any incorporated Society fhould have power by their charter, *to make alterations in their inftitution.* If this Society has any fuch, Mr. *Apthorp* was doubtlefs right in fpeaking of it as *a large difcretionary power!* For is not a power to make *alterations* in their inftitution, equivalent to a power to *alter their inftitution itfelf;*—to depart in a great meafure from the original plan according to the charter, and to purfue ends different from thofe which are expreffed therein? And what corporation ever had fo large a difcretionary power as this?

3. BY

3. By laying claim to fuch an extraordinary power for the Society, and making ufe of this as an argument to juftify their conduct, Mr. *Apthorp* feems to allow that they ftand in *need* of it for that purpofe. The gentleman furely would not have had recourfe to fuch a fuppofed wonderful power vefted in the Society, if their conduct could be reconciled with the moft plain, obvious fenfe of the charter.

4. THIS is, in effect, tho' not exprefly, a conceffion that the Society have actually made *alterations* in their inftitution : and have really been purfuing defigns not exprefly authorized by the charter. That this is fact, I am far from denying. But the gentleman well knows, that the queftions *de facto* and *de jure*, are very different: And if he can clear up that *of right*, as plainly as I flatter myfelf I have and fhall do that *of fact*, our debate will be half finifhed. But ftill it muft be remembered, that tho' the Society had confeffedly a power to make *alterations* in their inftitution, by neglecting fome ends thereof particularly mentioned in the charter, and purfuing others not mentioned ; yet unlefs they are fuppofed infallible and impeccable, *thefe alterations* may be for the *worfe*. That the alterations which they have made, are for the *better*, will not follow, as he feems to fuppofe, from their having had a *legal* power to make them. Allowing the power, if by altering they mend their inftitution, they are doubtlefs to be praifed in that refpect : But whatever power they may have, if they pejorate their inftitution,

inftitution, and purfue comparatively mean and
low ends, inftead of the noble ones expreffed in
the charter, Mr. *Apthorp* will not deny but that
this is an error of judgment at beft, and a real
abufe of their power. Whoever would fully
vindicate the Society, muft prove, not only that
they are actually invefted with fuch a power,
but that they have ufed it difcretely and wifely;
fo as moft effectually to anfwer the general and
excellent end of their inftitution : To alledge
power only in their vindication, is not giving
reafonable fatisfaction to thofe who may except
againft their conduct : Becaufe even a legal
power may be abufed, or a difcretionary power
mifapplied.   But,

5. THE charter contains no expreffion equivalent or fimilar to this, of a power left to the
Society *to make alterations in their inftitution.*
The ftrongeft expreffions ufed therein, relative
to the power given them, are thefe—" The faid
" Society fhall and may confult, determine, con-
" ftitute, ordain and make *any conftitutions, laws,*
" *ordinances and ftatutes* whatfoever ; as alfo
" execute leafes for years, as aforefaid, which to
" them, or the major part of them then prefent,
" fhall feem reafonable, profitable or requifite,
" for, touching or concerning the good eftate,
" rule, order and government of the faid cor-
" poration, *and the more effectual promoting the*
" *faid charitable defigns.*" Now is there any
thing here, that is in the leaft fimilar to a power
of making *alterations in their inftitution ?*—or
a right to apply their fund in any manner whatever, not expreffed in their charter ? So far
from it, that,   6. THE

6. THE Society are, by this very part of the charter which, it is pretended, gives them fuch an extraordinary power, limited and confined to thofe ends or objeĉts, which had before been exprefly mentioned as the ends of the inftitution. For the power here granted them to make conftitutions, laws, &c. is, in exprefs terms, in order to " the more effeĉtual promoting *the faid charitable defigns.*" And what, in the name of *charity*, are they? Is any one of them, the fupporting and increafing little epifcopal parties and faĉtions in thofe colonies, where due and legal provifion was before made for the public worfhip of God; and where the people " had the means of religion already, in other *proteftant communions?*"—and this to the manifeft prejudice of thofe colonies in which no fuch provifion was made for the adminiftration of God's word and ordinances;—of the Negro flaves and Savages! I afk again, whether this is one of *the faid charitable defigns?* If it is, then the Society have unqueftionably a right to make conftitutions, laws, &c. in order to *the more effeĉtual promoting it:* But if not, what can be lefs pertinent and fatisfaĉtory, than to alledge the large difcretionary power given them, to juftify their conduĉt in this refpeĉt? And how did this *inventive* gentleman come to talk of a power *to make alterations in their inftitution?* What that inftitution is, and all the ends of it, have been fufficiently explained before: And whatever they are, the Society are here confined, limited and tied down to them, as much as if they had
again

again been enumerated in the very words of the preamble ; to which the reader is referred. The Society muſt indeed, in the nature of the thing, if they act with ſimplicity and integrity in this important affair, act as to them ſhall ſeem moſt *reaſonable, profitable*, &c. in order to accompliſh *the ſaid deſigns* ; as other perſons intruſted with a diſcretionary power in order to accompliſh *certain ends*, muſt alſo act. But their *inſtitution itſelf is fixed*, immutably *fixed* by the charter ; ſo that they have not the leaſt power to make *alterations* in it ; but only to proſecute, in the moſt effectual manner, the declared ends of it. And if any incorporated charitable Society whatſoever, under the pretext of a diſcretionary power, neglect the declared ends of their inſtitution ; and purſue others, to which their charter is a ſtranger, they cannot but be conſidered as acting contrary to the truſt repoſed in them : But whether wilfully, or thro' miſapprehenſion, is another queſtion ; reſpecting which people may have different opinions. But,

7. HAS not the ingenious Mr. *Apthorp* a very ſingular way of reaſoning here ? He certainly makes uſe of a kind of *logic*, which very few of the *un-orthodox* N. England miniſters learnt at *our* little, young Colleges. For, having endeavoured to eſtabliſh this extraordinary diſcretionary power of the Society to make *alterations* in their inſtitution, as if all depended upon it ; the triumphant concluſion at length comes out in the following words : " THUS, with an *evidence*

S   " *beyond*

" *beyond exception*, it appears, that their conduct
" in placing churches AMONG US, *is in all res-*
" *pects* CONFORMABLE TO THEIR INSTITU-
" TION"— i. e. becaufe he had made it fo evident, that they had power to make ALTERA-
TIONS in their inftitution; therefore they have
made NONE, nor in the leaft deviated from it ;
but their conduct is in *all refpects* CONFORMA-
BLE thereto ! And this, it is faid, appears from
the premifes, *with an evidence beyond exception*—
But if their conduct is thus conformable to their
inftitution, why did Mr. *Apthorp* attempt to
juftify it, by afferting their power to *alter* their
inftitution ? As his argument now ftands, the
premifes and the conclufion unluckily frown on,
and militate againft each other. I have try'd
feveral ways to reconcile them ; but to no purpofe. I have endeavoured to fuppofe, that this
pofition about the large difcretionary power of
the Society, was bro't in only as Mr. *Apthorp*
fays, *Indian converfions are undertaken by the*
Society, viz. " incidentally, and as it were *ex-*
" *abundanti* †". But ftill, either the conclufion
knocks down the premifes, or the premifes the
conclufion. I have alfo endeavoured to fuppofe
the ingenious gentleman's meaning was, that the
Society's conduct was conformable to their inftitution, *after they had made alterations in it*, by
virtue of their " large difcretionary power"; not
as it was *originally :* But neither can I make this
bear, in feveral refpects. The war ftill continues
between

† *Confideration,* p. 15.

between the former and latter branch of the argument: So that they muſt be left to fight it out betwixt them.

XXXXXXXXXXXXXXXX!XXXXXXXXXXXXXX

SECTION XX.

Remarks on Mr Apthorp's *curious Application of thoſe Words,* Is it not lawful for me to do what I will with mine own? *&c. to the preſent Controverſy.*

IMMEDIATELY after the paſſage laſt quoted, Mr. *Apthorp,* that he might oblige us with ſome of his *rhetoric* together with his *invincible arguments,* ſubjoins— " And to any one who " cries out on *imaginary* abuſes or miſapplicati- " ons, the Society may reply, like the good " *Houſholder* whoſe *ſtewards* they are, *Is it* " *not lawful for me to do what I will with mine* " *own? is thine eye evil becauſe I am good?* "

LET it here be obſerved,

1. THAT whatever the Society might juſtly reply to thoſe who cry out on *imaginary abuſes* or *miſapplications;* the ſame reply would not be valid or pertinent to thoſe who cry out on *real* ones.

2. THE Society are here very juſtly ſtiled *ſtewards.* And they were intruſted with the care of a charitable fund, not only by God, as he ſeems to

intend,

intend, but by men ; by the King, who granted their charter, and by all who have contributed to the charitable deſigns expreſſed therein.

3. A LEARNED clergyman, like him, doubt-leſs knows, it is " required in *ſtewards* that a man be found *faithful*." Stewards are not al-lowed to uſe the goods or money with which they are intruſted, but for thoſe ends and pur-poſes for which they are committed to them. If they knowingly apply them to any others, how-ever good in themſelves, they are unfaithful in their truſt. For example, if a ſteward is intruſted with money by his lord, to give to particular poor perſons by name, or to the poor of ſuch a pariſh ; and he neglects theſe, to relieve other perſons, tho' equally neceſſitous, he miſapplies the money, and abuſes his truſt : Much more ſo, if inſtead of beſtowing it on *any* of the poor, he employs it in building and decorating an houſe *for himſelf*, and in adorning his wife, miſſes or children.

4. THAT the Society have applied a great part of the money intruſted with them, to other, and to ſay the leaſt, much leſs noble purpoſes than thoſe for which it was committed to them, has, if I miſtake not, been ſufficiently proved.

5. IN the very ſame ſentence that Mr. *Ap-thorp* calls the Society *ſtewards*, he does, in effect, ſuppoſe them to be, not *ſtewards*, but *lords* or *proprietors*. For he ſuppoſes them to have an abſolute, uncontroulable right to apply their cha-ritable fund to whatever good uſes they pleaſe.
This

This he evidently does, by putting that reply of
the *good Houſholder*, the *Proprietor* and *Lord
of all*, into their mouths, to ſtop the mouths of
thoſe who cry out on abuſes and miſapplications
—" Is it not lawful for me to do what I
" will with *mine own? is thine eye evil*, becauſe
" *I am good?*" This anſwer could with no propriety be adopted by a *ſteward*, when accuſed or
ſuſpected of abuſing his truſt, and alienating the
money committed to him from the particular
deſigns of it. The language is ſutable only to a
proprietor, at abſolute liberty to diſpoſe of *his
own goods* as he pleaſes, without being obliged
to give an *account* of his conduct ; as the Society
expreſly are, by their charter—" The ſaid Socie-
" ty ſhall yearly, and every year, *give an account*
" in writing", &c. And is it not a little ſingular,
that this argumentative and rhetorical gentleman
ſhould thus, in the ſame breath, make the Society
both *ſtewards* and ſovereign *proprietors* of the
charitable fund in their hands ?—characters ab-
ſolutely incompatible with each other in the ſame
perſons, and with relation to the ſame thing ; as
he applies them to the Society, " to convince the
" candid", and all but " the obſtinate" and
" malicious"; which, he ſays, " is not in the
" *power of reaſon.*"

6. Tho' the members of the Society are
themſelves large *contributers* to this fund, it
makes no material alteration in the caſe. Whatever they ſubſcribe or contribute, ceaſes to be
their own, their private property, as ſoon as it is
                                              put

put into this common ſtock. It is then no longer *their own*, to uſe as they pleaſe, or to alienate from the particular charitable ends mentioned in their charter. This were *ſacrilege* in a
much more proper ſenſe than that, in which the
epiſcopal clergy have termed ſome *other aliena-
tions* ſacrilege. And ſuppoſing ſuch an unjuſt
thing to be *deſignedly* done, which I am not
willing to think, the words of the apoſtle to
ANANIAS, who kept back part of the price, &c.
would be very applicable to this caſe— " Why
" hath Satan filled thine heart to lie to the holy
" Ghoſt, and to keep back part of the price of
" the land? *Whiles it remained*, was it not
" *thine own?*——Thou haſt not lied unto men
" [only] but unto God".—Let me juſt add here,
that if the *eye* of any one is *evil* towards the
Society, poſſibly ſome better reaſon may be given
for it than this, that they are *good;* which were,
in divers reſpects, the worſt that could be aſſign-
ed—: at leaſt,it may not be, becauſe they are *too
good* to the colonies which *moſt need* their charity ;
or to the Negroes and Savages, who are the proper objects of it. †

† If the *other* London Society, or Scotch Society acted thus ; —
neglecting the heathens, and heatheniſh places, to ſupport aud
increaſe little *presbyterian* parties where due proviſion was made
for the worſhip of God in the epiſcopal way ; epiſcopalians would
hardly be ſatisfied with this anſwer, that they *might do what they
would with their own.* They would be cenſured as bigots, influenced by the ſpirit of party, and perverting their fund.

SECTION

SECTION XXI.

Of the Plea, That the episcopal Missions in the Colonies, to rectify the State of Religion in them, are a necessary Means *of christianizing the Savages.*

THIS is often mentioned in the *Abstracts ;* and has not seldom served as a theme · for popular declamation in the anniversary sermons. Mr. *Apthorp* has quoted, or at least pretended to quote, several of those sermons to this purpose. I have compared but one of these quotations with the text itself ; that from the bp. of St. David's sermon ; (*Consid.* p. 15.) In which short quotation of but eight lines, there are three or four deviations from the usual way of quoting. Some of his own words are inserted as the words of the sermon ; clauses are left out, and parts of sentences at the distance of 13 pages in quarto are tacked together, and pointed as they ought to have been, if they had been contiguous in the sermon ; tho' the pages from whence they are taken, are indeed referred to in the margin. How he has used some other authors from whom he quotes ; and even that great Prelate who " presides over the church of England, *and the Society itself,*" I have not thought it worth while to examine. He has not indeed misrepresented the sense of the bp. of St. David's sermon ; and perhaps not that of other bps, &c.

as

as to this point. For I know it is a uſual thing for the preachers before the Society to talk in the ſame ſtrain, about " remedying in the firſt " place, *the ill ſtate of religion in our colonies* " *themſelves :*" without which care, it is ſaid, " the converſion of the neighbouring Savages " can hardly be effected ;" and the like.

LET it be here obſerved,

1. THAT all this kind of reaſoning ſuppoſes, that one principal object of the Society, is, the converſion of the Savages ; and ſo does not well harmonize with what Mr. *Apthorp* ſays elſe-where, however true in point of fact— " *Indian* " *converſions are undertaken by our Society* " *incidentally*, and as it were *ex abundanti.*"

2. THIS reaſoning.ſeems very juſt, when ap-plied to *moſt* of the Britiſh colonies, and the miſſions in them ; *viz.* all thoſe, the religious, or rather irreligious ſtate of which, anſwers to the repreſentations in the charter ;—thoſe colo-nies in which no tolerable proviſion was before made for miniſters ;—in which the people ſeem-ed abandoned to atheiſm and infidelity, or in danger of being perverted to popery, for want of the adminiſtration of God's word and ſacra-ments. Sending miſſionaries to ſuch places as theſe, is doubtleſs one proper means of propa-gating Chriſtianity among the heathen. But,

3. NOTHING can well be leſs to the purpoſe than this kind of reaſoning, when applied to the far greater part of N. England, where the pub-lick worſhip of God was ſo regularly upheld,
and

and the people "had the means of religion al-
" ready, in other *proteſtant communions.*" Such
expreſſions as thoſe, of *remedying the ill ſtate of
religion in the colonies,* and the like ; when applied to the Maſſachuſetts and Connecticut, can
naturally import nothing more than reducing
us to an outward *uniformity* of profeſſion, or
converting us to epiſcopacy and the liturgy.
But ſuppoſing this to be done, it is not eaſy to
ſee how it would contribute much to the converſion of the Indians. Nay, if we conſider
what has been done hitherto to this end, by
epiſcopalians and preſbyterians, &c. reſpectively ; there is great reaſon to think that our
converſion to the church of England would
rather retard than promote the converſion of
the Savages. And it is intimated even in ſome
of the anniverſary ſermons before the Society,
that the people of New-England had *provoked
them to jealouſy* in this reſpect ; tho' hitherto, to
very little purpoſe. Thus particularly biſhop
BURNET ſays, " Let thoſe who have a true
" zeal for the honor of *our church,* contribute
" to raiſe her glory, which hitherto has been
" *too little advanced this way,* while thoſe who
" *divide from us in* NEW-ENGLAND, ſeem to
" have provok'd us to *jealouſy* on this ac-
" count."† Similar conceſſions to our honor,
might be produced from other anniverſary
ſermons.

T   4. As

Sermon before the Soc. p. 27.

4. As the converfion of the heathen was from the firft one profeffed aim of our Fore-fathers in fettling in New-England ; fo almoft all the royal charters, grants, letters patent, and acts of government in England, relative to this country, have made mention of, and encouraged, yea, enjoined upon us the profecution of this pious defign ; not confidered as epifcopalians, but as known diffenters from the Englifh church. To which purpofe is the following paffage in the charter of this province, granted in the 12th of WILLIAM and MARY ; the year before the Society's charter — " To difpofe of matters and things
" whereby our fubjects, inhabitants of our
" faid province, may be religioufly, peacea-
" bly and civily governed, protected and de-
" fended ; fo as their good life, and orderly
" converfation may win the *Indians*, natives
" of the country, to the knowledge and obe-
" dience of the only true God and Saviour of
" mankind, and the Chriftian faith ; which
" his royal Majefty our royal Grandfather K.
" CHARLES the firft, in his faid letters patent,
" declared was *his royal intention*, and the
" *adventurers free profeffion to be the principal*
" *end of the faid plantation.* And for the better
" maintaining and fecuring *liberty of confcience*,
" &c. "

5. CAN it be reafonably fuppofed that King WILLIAM, in the Society's charter granted the year after this, had the leaft thoughts of im-

impowering them to employ a great part of
their fund in converting us to epifcopacy, and
uniformity in worfhip, either as one *end* of
their inftitution, or as a requifite *means* of converting the Indians ;—a pious work all along
recommended to, and enjoined upon the inhabitants of New-England themfelves ! The
royal charters, letters patent, grants, &c. fuppofe the fettlers and inhabitants of this country, tho' not epifcopalians, to have been a religious people, who were difpofed and qualified to ferve the interefts of religion, by chriftianizing the Indians. But it feems Mr. *Apthorp,* not to fay, the Society, think that, inftead of confining their pious care to the heathenifh colonies, or applying themfelves directly to the Indians, they are to employ a
great part of their fund in converting us to the
liturgy, as a *neceffary means* of converting the
Savages. Is this fuch a method of juftifying
the New-England miffions, as muft needs
" convince the candid ?"—*confute* all but the
" obftinate," and *filence* all but the " malici-
" ous !"

6. Upon fuppofition that our converfion to
epifcopacy had really fome *remote tendency* towards the converfion of the Indians to the
faith of Chrift ; (which is utterly denied) yet
it may well be doubted, whether this would
juftify the Society in applying fo great a part
of their fund for the fupport and increafe of
the epifcopal party here, in a country whofe

T 2   religious

religious ftate no ways anfwers to the defcrip-
tions in the charter ; to the negleƈt of other
colonies, and the heathen themfelves, the di-
reƈt, proper objeƈts of their charity. Colonies
whofe religious ftate is like that of the Maffachufets and Conneƈticut, are implicitly exclu-
ded from any fhare in this charity, by the reprefentations given in the charter, of thofe for
which it was defigned, fo widely different
therefrom. And to bring in thefe New-England miffions and miffionaries thus *indireƈtly*, or
edge-ways, as a pretended *means* of converting
the Savages, when they cannot be juftified *di-*
reƈtly, by the exprefs, obvious defign of the
charter ; is no better than an evafion ; and
one that naturally brings to mind thofe words
of the CHIEF SHEPHERD, fo often mifapplied by epifcopalians—" He that entereth not
" *by the door*, into the fheepfold, but climbeth
" up *fome other way*, the fame is a thief and a
" robber."—Tho' I do not mean to call the
Society's miffionaries among us, by thofe opprobrious names ; or to give them any perfonal affront.   But,

7. IF it fhould be faid, that *any means* which
have even a remote tendency to the converfion of the Indians, may be ufed by the Society to that *end*, by virtue of their " large
difcretionary power ;" and if it is upon this
footing that the miffions here are juftified,
let us confider how far the fame way of reafoning might carry them, and where it would
                                          end.

end. They think our converfion to epifcopacy a means of converting the Indians. They
are therefore, in purfuance of the maxim a-
forefaid, right in maintaining miffions here at
a great annual expence, with the hopes of
thrufting in the fickle, and reaping a mighty
Indian harveft a century or two hence, when
it is ripened by means of the benign influences
of epifcopacy upon New-England. Neither
I, indeed, nor probably the reader, can fee
how this fuppofed means tends to the propofed end. It feems a round-about, aukward
way of going to work : But no matter ; the
Society judge it proper, and that is fufficient.
Let us then proceed one ftep farther. If the
church of Scotland, for which we have generally a great veneration, was but firft *epifcopized;*
this might poffibly have fome remote tendency to induce us to conform to the church of
England ; and therefore a tendency, according to the prefent fuppofition, tho' more remote, to convert the Indians. Now, if it
fhould appear thus to the Society, they may,
according to the maxim aforefaid, fend miffionaries to convert the kirk, in order to the
converfion of New-England ; and this in order to convert the Savages on our frontiers.
With the fame pious defign, they might alfo
fend miffionaries into Holland, Geneva, the
Swifs Cantons, &c. For though the charter
fays nothing of Scotland, Holland, Geneva,
Switzerland, or even of New-England, but
implicitly

implicitly excludes them all from the charitable care of the Society ; yet the Society, it is said, have a *large diſcretionary power,—even occaſionally to make alterations in their inſtitution, in ſuch a manner as to render it moſt beneficial to religion, whether in our colonies, or among the bordering nations.*—Who then can doubt the right of the Society to maintain miſſions in all the proteſtant countries of Europe, to promote the peculiarities of the church of England, in order to the eſtabliſhing of epiſcopacy and uniformity among us ; and to *remedy the ill ſtate of religion here*, without which, " the conver-" ſion of the neighbouring Savages can hard-" ly be effected ! " — Now, where Mr. *Apthorp's* method of reaſoning, joined with ſuch an *imagination*, may end, it is not eaſy to ſay ; except perhaps in the Society's appointing proper perſons to look out for ſome Geeſe of the breed of GONSALES, to carry miſſionaries to the moon, in order to convert the *good man* there to the church, in order to his coming as an apoſtle to convert us ; and all this as a *means* of converting the *Iroquois*, &c. And indeed, conſidering how ſcriptural our religion is at preſent ; and how unlikely we are to better ourſelves by ſo great a change, either on temporal or ſpiritual accounts ; it may be hoped that we ſhall not be generally epiſcopized in a long time, unleſs that officious planet, at leaſt by ſome ſecret and powerful *influence*, ſhould have a conſiderable hand in the apoſtolical work of our converſion.   IF

IF this is too ludicrous for the grave reader, I afk his pardon. To be ferious, is it not a furprifing thing, that the Society fhould expend large fums annually for half a century together, in order to eftablifh epifcopacy among us, under the poor, thin pretext of its being a neceffary *means* of converting the Indians?— and at the fame time neglect, in fo great a degree, both the Indians themfelves, and thofe heathenifh colonies, which are the proper, direct objects of their inftitution! Can any fuppofed *difcretionary power*, however *large*, poffibly juftify a conduct fo aliene from the obvious fenfe, letter, and whole fpirit of their charter?

╬╬╬╬╬╬╬╬╬╬╬╬╬╬╬╬╬╬╬╬╬╬╬

SECTION XXII.

Remarks on a curious Argument of Mr. Apthorp, *in favor of* the Church of England.

IT was by no means my defign, in this publication, to enter into the controverfy betwixt the church of England and us. But as Mr. *Apthorp* has thought fit to produce an argument in favor of the former, in the margin of the 22ᵈ and 23ᵈ pages of the *Confiderations*, I cannot but take a curfory notice of it. " It " is,

" is a *good* prefumption," fays he, " that the
" church of England is a reafonable Chriftian
" communion, and free from all extremes in
" its conftitution ; that all the various religi-
" ous perfuafions, at home and abroad, con-
" cur in holding it *next* in efteem to their own.
" Confidering the force of prejudice, what in
" every one's judgment holds the *fecond place*,
" may be fuppofed to deferve *the firft*." The
ingenious gentleman adds, that " for this ob-
" fervation, *as far as he can recollect*, he is in-
" debted to a *fine writer*, Dr. JOHN BROWN"—
Be that as it may, I can give a guefs from
whence it came originally ; *viz.* from another
learned Divine of the church of England ; I
mean Dr. SWIFT.. For in his Dedication of
of that curious *theological production*, entitled
A TALE OF A TUB, are thefe words ; —
" It is a maxim, that thofe, to whom every
" body allows the *fecond place*, have an un-
" doubted title to the *firft*." This he applies, in
the way of *compliment*, to Lord SOMMERS.

BUT as to the obfervation itfelf, as applied
in a *compliment* to THE CHURCH ; where did
either of thefe gentlemen get his intelligence,
that ALL *the various religious perfuafions, at home
and abroad, concur in holding the church of England*
NEXT *in efteem to their own ?* Have they ex-
plicitly declared fo ? Have the churches of
Scotland, Holland, Geneva, the proteftant Swifs
Cantons ? have the Lutheran and Greek churches, &c, &c. by any folemn public act, pro-
claimed

claimed the church of England *second best* ? Or
has Mr. *Apthorp* the faculty of difcerning the
fentiments of all other churches, without their
declaring them ? Till this fact is well eftablifhed, the argument which he deduces from it
may well be called a *prefumption* ; but, that it is
a *good* one, as he fays, is not fo evident.——
There is indeed *one church*, a very *ancient* and
extenfive one, which, it may naturally be con-
cluded, for a reafon that fhall be namelefs,
confiders the communion of the church of
England as the *next beft* to her own. But
it may well be doubted, whether one half the
proteftant churches in the world concur with
her, in holding the church of England in *fuch
high efteem.* And tho' this unfupported fuppofition were a certain fact ; yet it would be
no proper evidence that the church of England *is a reafonable Chriftian communion, and free
from all extremes in its conftitution,* with thofe
who plainly fee many unreafonable, unchrif-
tian, and unfcriptural extremes in her conftitution, worfhip and difcipline : Which almoft
any man, tolerably free from the prejudices of
education, may eafily fee ; and which have,
in effect, been acknowledged and lamented
by many of the wifeft and beft men of that
communion ; who would have been glad of
a farther reformation with refpect to thofe
*extremes.** U The

* The judicious, epifcopalian Authors of the *Free and candid
Difquifitions relating to the church of England,* fay, " The
" reformation

THE gentleman, by introducing this *good presumption*, as he calls it, tho' without foundation, in favor of the church of England, shews at least that he had not forgotten the great and important design of the Society's missions in these parts, *viz.* propagating the peculiarities of episcopacy, and reconciling us to the church of England. *Hic labor, hoc opus est.* What success the Society and missionaries may have in this favourite project, which engrosses so much of the attention, and absorbs so much of the revenues of the former, while it is almost the sole business of the latter; God only knows. But I have good reason to think that, in general, I speak the sense of far the greater, wiser and better part of the people in New-England in the following paragraph—

WHEN

" *reformation of* OUR CHURCH was never brought to that " perfection which the first undertakers and promoters of it " intended ; and which *many of the worthiest* of their suc- " ceffors have desired and pleaded for fince." Third Edit: *Dublin,* 1750. p. 246. They afterwards produce the testimony of great numbers of the most eminent bishops, and other learned men of the church of England, both clergy and laity, to support the assertion aforesaid. And they have themselves mentioned almost innumerable things, which they own to be very exceptionable in *their own church.* —— They also acknowledge, p. 344. that the learned Mr. *Pierce's* VINDICATION of the Dissenters " was never " answered, altho' somebody or other hath *attempted it* "— And if they had added, that it *never will*. nor *can be* answered, they had not gone too far. Indeed, these *Disquisitions* themselves contain one of the fullest and most unanswerable *Vindications* of our *dissent* from the church of England, that have appeared ; tho' *undesigned.*

WHEN we confider the real conftitution of the church of England ; and how aliene her mode of worfhip is from the fimplicity of the gofpel, and the apoftolic times : When we confider her enormous hierarchy, afcending by various gradations from the dirt to the fkies : When we confider the vifible effects of that church's prevailing among us to the degree that it has : When we reflect on what ourForefathers fuffered from the mitred, lordly SUCCESSORS *of the fifhermen of Galilee,* for non-conformity to a non-inftituted mode of worfhip ; which occafioned their flight into this weftern world : When we confider that, to be delivered from their unholy zeal and oppreffions, countenanced by fcepter'd tyrants, they threw themfelves as it were into the arms of Savages and Barbarians : When we reflect, that one principal motive to their exchanging the fair cities, villages, and delightful fields of Britain for the then inhofpitable fhores and defarts of America, was, that they might here enjoy, unmolefted, God's holy word and ordinances, without fuch heterogeneous and fpurious mixtures as were offenfive to their well-informed confciences : When we confider the narrow, cenforious and bitter fpirit that prevails in too many of the epifcopalians among us ; and what might probably be the fad confequence, if this growing party fhould once get the upper hand here, and a major vote in our houfes of *Affembly* : (in

which

which cafe the church of England might become the eftablifhed religion here ; *tefts* be
ordained, as in England, to exclude all but
conformifts from pofts of honor and emolu-
ment ; and all of us be taxed for the fupport
of *bifhops* and their *underlings* :) When we
confider thefe things, and too many others
to be now mentioned, we cannot well think
of that church's gaining ground here to any
great degree, and efpecially of feeing bifhop's
fixed among us, without much reluctance—
Will they never let us reft in peace, except
where all the weary are at reft? Is it not
enough, that they perfecuted us out of the
old world ? Will they purfue us into the new
to convert us here ? — *compaffing fea and land
to make us profelytes*, while they neglect the
heathen and heathenifh plantations ! What
other new world remains as a fanctuary for
us from their oppreffions, in cafe of need ?
Where is the COLUMBUS to explore one for,
and pilot us to it, before we are confumed by
the flames, or deluged in a flood of epifcopacy ? — For my own part, I can hardly ever
think of our being purfued thus from Britain
into the wilds of America, and from world to
world, without calling to mind, tho' without
applying, that paffage in the *Revelation* of St.
JOHN : " And to the woman were given two
" wings of a great eagle, that fhe might fly
" into the *wildernefs*, into *her place* ; where
" fhe is nourifhed — from the face of the fer-
" pent.

" pent.   And the ferpent caft out of his
" mouth water as a flood, after the woman ;
" that he might caufe her to be carried away
" of the flood. "

One of our Kings, it is well known, exci-
ted his Scotch fubjects to take up arms againft
him, in a great meafure, if not chiefly, by
attempting to force the Englifh liturgy upon
them, at the inftigation of the furious epifcopal zealots of that day ; by whom he was
wheedled and duped to his deftruction.   But
GOD be praifed, we have a KING, whom
Heaven long preferve and profper, too wife,
juft and good to be put upon any violent
meafures, to gratify men of fuch a depraved
turn of mind.—It is not my defign, however,
to difhonor the more moderate and Chriftian
fpirit of the Englifh bifhops fince the Revolution, particularly of this day, by comparing it to the perfecuting, anti-chriftian fpirit
of many prelates, antecedent to that glorious
Æra of Britifh liberty.

SECTION

SECTION XXIII.

Part of two letters *of Sir* WILLIAM ASHURST, Knight *and* Alderman, *relative to the* Society ; *with ſhort Remarks on them.*

THE author has in his hands two original letters of Sir WILLIAM ASHURST, Preſident of the *Society for propagating the goſpel in New-England and the parts adjacent in America* ; of which Dr. DOUGLASS ſays, " The whole revenue of the corporation " is £. 500 to £. 600 *ſterling* per Annum. At " preſent they exhibit *ſmall,* but *well placed* " *ſalaries* to ſeveral miſſionaries, Engliſh and " Indians."†— Theſe letters of Sir WILLIAM were written to a perſon in Boſton, concerning the affairs of *that Society* ; but contain ſome ſtrictures on *the other* ; by which it appears how early it was ſuſpected, that their views were not altogether ſo public-ſpirited and catholic, as might have been wiſhed. The firſt of them is dated, London, Auguſt 5, 1704. and contains the remarkable words following— " We have lately had a *new* Corpo- " ration erected here *for propagating the goſpel,* " &c.

† *Summ. Hiſt. and Political, &c.* Vol. II. pag. 122.

THE Author's Father was more than 60 years a preacher of the goſpel to the *Indians* ; employed by the *Commiſſioners* of this Society.

" &c. among the *epifcopal clergy.* In my laft
" letters in March, I fent Mr. SEWALL a
" fcheme of their proceedings. I envy not
" their engaging in fo pious a defign, but hear-
" ti'y with them all imaginable fuccefs. But
" their *firft fteps difcrver no great deal of charity*
" *for their fellow Chriftians.* For they would
" infinuate, that WE have *no minifters* employ-
" ed in this *converfion work* in America ; and
" therefore I cannot *expect much from them.*
" I doubt not but thofe employed by US are as
" good minifters as the *beft of them,* (tho' they
" have not epifcopal ordination) and may be
" fitter to be employed in this work," &c.

THE other letter bears date Auguft 10,
1714. and contains the following paffage—.
" It is a great rejoicing to us, to hear from
" you of the fuccefs that *our* endeavours have
" had amongft thofe poor people ; [i. e. the
" *Indians*] and I heartily wifh *the Society you*
" *take notice of* had made *greater improvements*
" *of the advantages they have over us.* But I
" am afraid God will not blefs their endea-
" vors ; they having neither *right ends in their*
" *view,* nor employing *proper inftruments* in
" the work. To propagate the Chriftian re-
" ligion *in its purity and fimplicity,* is an hea-
" venly work ; but to make it only a color to
" *aggrandize the hierarchy,* and to promote the
" intereft and glory of what they call *The*
" *church,* cannot either be called *a good work,*
" nor can *expect a bleffing upon it.*"—

WHETEHR

WHETHER the conduct of the Society since these letters were written, and the series of facts relative thereto, do not prove to a demonstration, that the Society have been influenced by narrow, party, unworthy views in a *great degree*; and consequently, that Sir WILLIAM was no ill prophet, is submitted to the judgment of the intelligent and impartial reader.

SECTION XXIV.

That by the Cession of Canada, *&c. there is now a noble* Prospect *of much being done towards christianizing the* Indians, *provided this* good Work *is heartily and discretely prosecuted.*

WHAT is past cannot be recalled, or undone: But abuses may be reformed, if the authors should be sensible of them, and not *above* altering their measures. The cession of Canada and the best part of Louisiana, if confirmed to Great-Britain, will give the several religious and charitable Societies in England, Scotland and New-England, erected for promoting the *common cause of Christianity*, advantages for spreading the gospel among the heathen in America, much superior to what they would otherwise be. And tho' some of the *political* reasons for attempting

ing the converfion of the Indians, may not
be altogether fo ftrong as they were, while
we had the French fo near us for rivals and
enemies on this continent ; yet all the obligations arifing from *humanity, piety* and *charity*
remain in their full force. Yea, thefe are really heightened in the fame degree that obftacles to this good work are removed out of the
way. It may be naturally expected that the
Indians will be more acceffible and tractable
to us and our miffionaries, by reafon of the fall
of Canada, and the French power in America,
than they were before, either to us or to
the French ; as they will now be rather more
dependent upon us. Thefe circumftances, of
fuch great importance to the profperity of the
Britifh colonies, and to Great Britain herfelf,
may well be confidered as a loud *call of pro-*
vidence to her and them, to engage heartily in
the bufinefs of chriftianizing the Natives :
And the religious obligation hereto, increafes
in proportion to the profpect, or probability of
fuccefs in the attempt ; as was hinted before.

THERE is no reafon to doubt, from any
thing that is paft, but that the Societies referred
to before, *excepting one,* will be forward to
improve the opportunity, and all advantages
which God in his providence affords, for
fpreading the knowledge of his truth, and the
common falvation among the American Savages.
And fo far as *words* and *profeffions* can go,—even
the moft folemn, and addreffed to the greateft
W perfonages,

perfonages, there is the ftrongeft reafon to conclude that *that Society* will not neglect fo fair an
opportunity as is now prefented to them, for
propagating Chriftianity among thefe nations.
For *the Society for propagating the gofpel in foreign parts,*in their *addrefs* to His Majefty, 1760,
prefented by the Archbifhop of Canterbury,
exprefs themfelves thus—" This Society was
" wifely founded by our great deliverer King
" Wᴵᴸᴸᴵᴀᴹ, that the *remoteft of the plantations,*
" by the inftruction of an orthodox clergy,
" might be preferved from the danger of *in-*
" *fidelity,* and guarded againft the reftlefs at-
" tempts of *popery ;* and that the pure light of
" the *gofpel* might be fpread amongft *thofe a-*
" *round them,* who fat in the darknefs of *hea-*
" *thenifm.* The glorious acquifitions which
" have *enlarged your Majefty's empire in Ame-*
" *rica, open a yet more extenfive field for our at-*
" *tention and care.* And we do ʜᴜᴍʙʟʏ ᴀɴᴅ
" ꜱᴏʟᴇᴍɴʟʏ ᴀꜱꜱᴜʀᴇ your Majefty, that, fo
" far as our ability reaches,——we will exert
" our *utmoft endeavours,* that no part of your
" Majefty's dominions *for which our duty calls*
" *us to provide,* may remain unfurnifhed with
" the means of being inftructed in *genuine*
" *Chriftianity :* and will ɢᴏ ᴏɴ" [*Quere,* Whether this fhould not rather have been, ʙᴇɢɪɴ]
" to ftudy and *ufe diligently* the moft probable
" methods of *converting,* not only the Nᴇ-
" ɢʀᴏ ꜱʟᴀᴠᴇꜱ, but the neighbouring Iɴ-
" ᴅɪᴀɴꜱ."†

Iᴛ

† Vid. *Scots Magazine : Appendix,* 1760. p. 693.

IT is to be hoped that the venerable Society will not forget thefe SOLEMN ASSURANCES, as they *feem* to have forgotten others fimilar to them in times paft ; and *go on* to mifapply large fums annually, for fupporting and increafing the epifcopal party or faction in New-England, inftead of *ufing diligently the moft probable methods of* CONVERTING *either the* NEGRO SLAVES *or neighbouring* INDIANS. If Indian converfions have hitherto been undertaken by the Society only " incidentally, and as it were *ex abundanti,* " as Mr. *Apthorp* fays ; yet it may be expected that, after thefe proteftations, they will undertake them in a different manner ; with more zeal and vigor, and a lefs fparing hand as to money ; curtailing their fuperfluous expences in the Maffachufets and Connecticut, † where their affiftance is not needed to fave US from atheifm, infidelity or popery ; where

" Non tali auxilio, nec defenforibus iftis
Tempus eget"—

Or if their *memory* fhould be treacherous, it may be hoped there will not be wanting thofe about his Majefty's perfon, to *remind* them of their *humble and folemn affurances to* HIM : Efpecially fince their *non-obfervance* of them may prove of very pernicious confequence, not only to His American dominions, but to Great-Britain. Of which in the following fection.

W 2   SECTION

---

† The author has, within a few days, been informed, that in the province of *New-Hampfhire* there is a legal provifion made for the fupport of a public religion, fimilar to that in thofe two other New-England governments.

SECTION XXV.

Of the political *Reasons* still remaining, *for endeavouring to christianize the* Indians.

SOME people may perhaps imagine, that since the cession of Canada, &c. there are no motives or reason besides merely *religious* ones, to attempt the civilizing and converting the American Indians. That the *political* ones which before subsisted, are *lessened* in some degree, is not denied ; but, that they are wholly *ceased*, no one who duly considers the matter, can suppose.

To say nothing of the benefits that might result herefrom to the agriculture, fishery and navigation of the colonies, and to the British commerce, even upon supposition that there was not a jesuit, popish priest, emissary, or one Frenchman upon this continent ; it is to be remembred, that *human affairs* are subject to great changes and revolutions, as we have lately seen, particularly in America. We cannot be *certain* that others may no take place hereafter, almost as much to our prejudice, as those are to our advantage. At least, human prudence requires that every thing of that sort should be guarded against, as far as human foresight and power can do it. And one means hereof doubtless is, using the present opportunity of spreading, as far as may be, the Christian, protestant religion among the Natives ; and thereby engag-
ing

ing them *heartily* in the Britifh intereft, in oppofition to the French.

THE French are a very powerful and politic,
ambitious and enterprifing nation : They do
not long fit down eafy under *great loffes* ; and
they foon recover themfelves by peace, after being
exhaufted by war. In all probability, they will
continue to carry on intrigues with the Indians
of Canada, and on the Eaft of the Miffifippi, by
means of their emiffaries, to the prejudice of our
colonies ; not without hopes of finding their
ends in it at left—The reverend and learned
EDWARD WIGGLESWORTH, D. D. HOLLI-
SIAN † Profeffor of divinity at Harvard College
in Cambridge, who has thought much and long
on the affair of the miffions and the Indians,
has obliged me with two or three letters fince I
have been writing on this fubject. In one of
them (which I obtained his leave to make ufe
of on this occafion) he fpeaks particularly of
what has laft been hinted at. And, I conceive,
the beft ufe I can make of it, is to give the public the fubftance of it in the Doctor's *own
words*, as follows.

——" Probably it may now be generally
" thought, that fince Canada is reduced, nothing
" more is to be apprehended from the Indians ;
" but that we fhall live in perpetual peace and
" good neighbourhood with them. Tho' it
" may be thought a weaknefs, I muft own, that
" I entertain very different apprehenfions. I
" believe

† N. B. This *Profefforfhip* was in great part endow'd by the
worthy Mr. THOMAS HOLLIS of London, fome time fince
deceafed ; a very generous benefactor to our College.
The prefent worthy THOMAS HOLLIS of London, *Efq*;
F. R. S. &c. has alfo, more than once, prefented fome valuable books to the library of faid College.

" believe that the French, in fpite of all precau-
" tions that can be taken, will continue miffion-
" aries among all thofe tribes of Indians, who
" have been ufed to have them ; and will thruft
" them into as many others as they poffibly can.
" One great bufinefs of thefe will be, to keep
" up a ftrong difaffection to the Englifh in the
" Savages, in hopes of making ufe of them, at
" fome future favourable conjuncture, to dif-
" trefs our provinces again, and recover their
" own loffes. To anfwer fuch an end, the
" French miffionaries will make no difficulty to
" drefs and paint like Savages, and pafs for as
" very Indians as any of them, even in vifits to
" our forts and frontier towns. And I know
" of nothing that can prevent fuch mifmanage-
" ments, but our having miffionaries among the
" Indians, who fhall be *men of genius enough to*
" *gain their efteem,* and *the fame afcendency over*
" *them,* which the French miffionaries get,
" wherever they come.

" If any fhould be fo fanguine as to flatter
" themfelves, that we fhall never again have *a*
" *weak adminiftration at home,* which may
" encourage the French to attempt to recover
" what they have loft in America ; yet we have
" found by experience, when Mr. Dummer
" commanded in chief, that by jefuitical influ-
" ence the Indians may be fpirited to make war
" upon us, even when the French *dare not ap-*
" *pear* to help or abet them. And if that war
" had not been conducted in a manner very
" different from the conduct of any other war
" we have ever had with our Eaftern tribes of
" Indians,

" Indians, before or fince; they would have
" been no more humbled then, than they ufed
" to be at other times; but might have con-
" tinued to harafs our borders, till we had
" been much more weary of the war than they.
" And if any tribes of Indians now fhould be fet
" on, by fecret French emiffaries among them,
" to ravage our new fettlements, and murder
" the inhabitants; I fufpect they might *live*
" *better by it than by hunting :* And they
" might [perhaps] be better fupplied with all
" they want, except money for our fcalps, *by*
" *fuch Englifh provinces as they were pleafed*
" *not to moleft*, than they ever were by the
" French in Canada."

THE preceeding extract is given, not only as
very clearly and precifely expreffing my own
apprehenfions ; but becaufe it is naturally con-
cluded, that coming from an *aged* gentleman,
of fo fuperior and refpectable a character as
Dr. WIGGLESWORTH, it will have a greater
attention paid to it, than the fame things coming
only from myfelf could have claimed. Let
me add; It is undoubted fact, that in fome
of our French and Indian wars, the Savages
have been fupplied even with *ammunition* from
one or more of the Britifh colonies: And it
has been reported, I believe truly, that the
cleaths of fome of our people, butchered by
them, have been very *amicably* fold at Albany,
with the blood upon them—In a word, the neceffity of having a confiderable number of
miffionaries among the Indians, is fo apparent
and urgent, in a political, as well as religious

consideration

conſideration of things; that one can hardly
help entertaining ſome hopes that the government, either at home or in America, or both,
may in their wiſdom ſee cauſe to do ſomething
towards ſending and ſuppoiting them : At leaſt,
that the ſeveral corporations erected in part, if
not chiefly for that very end, will purſue it with
a zeal adequate to the importance of it.

✻✻✻✻✻✻✻✻✻✻✻✻✻✻✻✻✻✻✻✻✻✻

SECTION XXVI.

*Containing ſome farther Strictures on the
Manner of Mr. Apthorp's conducting
his Defence of the Society.*

MR. *Apthorp's* defence of the Society is
entitled, " CONSIDERATIONS," &c.
And tho' it has not been thought
needful to follow him ſtep by ſtep ; yet, I flatter myſelf, enough has been ſaid to convince
the impartial, that thoſe *Conſiderations* were
both written and publiſhed with far too little
conſideration. He began his triumph, however,
or rather inſult, in the title-page, by a long,
ſcornful, moſt contemptuous *motto* ; in which
he intimates, how much beneath him he thought
it to enter the liſts with any perſon, who was ſo
hardy as to object againſt the Society; reproaching them all, in effect, as vain, impudent liars—
" Vanos continuò ac mendaces eſſe"— I his *reviling* motto, which ſerves him as an *exordium,* is
from the *Evangelical Preparation* of EUSEBIUS:
And

And on the other fide of the fame leaf are adver-
tized, " SERMONS on PRAYER, with FORMS of
" DEVOTION": which we may charitably fuppofe
defigned for *general* ufe ;—both for thofe who had
devotion before, without much *formality* ; and thofe
who had *formality* enough before, without much
devotion. Next appears his *humble fubmiffion* of
his defence, to the " judgment and decifion" of
his venerable *Clients,* the Society, of which he
is himfelf a *member.* In the firft page, (numbered
7) he propofes a queftion that is hardly intelligible ; fpeaks of it as very " interefting", and
modefly exprefles his intention to determine it
" *once for all'*—And this, without " the *leaft*
" intention of offence or *controverfy*", (p. 8.)
He alfo fays there, " The propofed vindication is
" defigned to convince the *candid.* To confute
" the *obftinate,* and filence the *malicious,* is not
" in the *power of reafon."* But, by the way, I
have always fuppofed that the *obftinate* were as
capable of being *confuted* by the *power of reafon,*
as others ; tho' much more hard to be *convinced,*
or put to *filence :* And I hope that this gentleman will never ferve as an example, to fhew the
wide difference betwixt thefe things, which he
now feems to confider as the fame. But be
that as it may,
"Quid dignum tanto feret hic PROMISSOR hiatu !"

IT appears that he was put upon this *defperate*
undertaking, by fomething which, it feems, had
offended him in a news-paper, relative to the
miffions. And p. 9. he threatens the unknown
author of a fuppofed infult on the *dead,* with

X   inftant

inftant deftruction from his powerful quill ; fay-
ing with the old Trojan Hero,

Extinxiffe nefas ——, et fumpfiffe merentis
Laudabor pœnas—

Confidering the *occafion*, I wonder he did not
adopt the next words alfo—

———————— Animumg ; expleffe juvabit
Ultricis flammæ, et *cineres* fatiaffe meorum.

And the following line may perhaps be proper
for a motto for him, if he fhould again write
on the fubject : *viz.*

Talia *jactabam*, et *furiatâ* mente ferebar.

But as he was to determine the matter *once for
all*, this is not to be expected.

FROM the 9th to the 18th p. we find him
chiefly employed, firft in *mifquoting*, and then
in *mifreprefenting* the charter ; in putting in an
exclufive claim to *orthodoxy* for the clergy of the
church of England ; making the Society *ftewards*
and fovereign *proprietors*, in the fame breath ;
reproaching others with " great ignorance, or
fomething *worfe*"; reviling the religion of our
Forefathers in the moft opprobrious terms ; and
fhewing how *greatly* our reformation in religion,—without the improvement of our *morals* or
piety, is *the work of the Society*.

HAVING thus prepared the way, he propofes
(p. 18.) " to take leave of this popular objection
" [againft the Society] with *fo full a confutation*,
" that it will be *difingenuous* ever to advance it
" again." How is that to be done ?—Why, by
" *confidently* refting his *proof* on the unexceptio-
" nable *teftimony* of two—*"Prelates"*— ; both of
them

them members of the Society—Let us fee how
many *metamorphofes* they have already paft thro';
1ft. they were *Clients*, 2dly. *Judges*, 3dly. they
are *Witneffes* ; and all in the fame caufe, *their
own*. But then, they are moft *unexceptionable*
Witneffes—"incapable either of *miftake* or *mifre-*
" *prefentation* in a matter fo thoroughly known
" to them." And (p. 19) he fpeaks of the " in-
" vincible reafons" of one of them. So that
Mr. *Apthorp*'s fruitful imagination has produced another *metamorphofis*. It feems they are
now neither *Clients, Judges*, nor *Witneffes* ; but,
4ly. *Reafoners*, pleading their own caufe. What
they fay, whether called their *teftimony* or their
reafoning, has been taken notice of ; and others
may think for themfelves, whether it is *unan-
fwerable* and *invincible*, or not.

PAGE 23. Mr. *Apthorp*, as well he might,
makes an " apology for his undertaking to vin-
" dicate a Society, which is *above cenfure*, as it is
" *incapable of wrong motives*."—An extraordinary
Society indeed ! And furely fome *apology* was
needed for officioufly undertaking the defence
of a Society fo *incapable* of erring. So that he
has, in effect, infallible Clients, infallible Judges,
infallible Witneffes, and infallible Reafoners ; all
on the fame fide with his own infallible *Self*, and
all in the *fame perfons* ! Did ever any man undertake a more *needlefs* work ! He feems indeed to
repent ; and " promifes, in amends, to employ
" his *ftudies*, for the future, *to better purpofes*,"
(p. 23.) Upon which *condition*, I think he ought
to be *forgiven* ; and, all things confidered, I know

X 2   of

of none fo *unlikely* to overlook his officious error, as the Society *themfelves*—But it would feem hard, not to fhew fome lenity to him ; efpecially if, as he there fays, " This bufinefs, in truth, was *forced* " upon him"—In fuch a cafe, whofe *ftars* could poffibly *prevent their writing* ; if they will but make the fad cafe their own ! This *force*, it feems, was chiefly put upon him by a Braintree gentleman, who, as he fuppofes, had infulted the memory of a deceafed miffionary ; and " by the honor " *done him* of *fharing* in the infult" ; as he has accurately expreffed it. He is very fevere on the faid Braintree gentleman : Whom, however, I fhould think almoft as *inhuman* and *barbarous* as he has been reprefented, if he defired any feverer revenge on Mr. *Apthorp*, than that *he fhould write more* SUCH CONSIDERATIONS and DE-FENCES.

Mr. *Apthorp* then paffes fome other *compliments* of a pretty *extraordinary nature*, however juft, on the Society, " the honor of our age and nati-" on," &c. Thefe might poffibly, however, have come from fome *other perfon* with as good a grace, as from a *member* of the Society ; accord-ing to that old maxim, ". Let another praife thee, " and *not thine own mouth*." He then gives it as his opinion, that the Society " cannot better " apply their munificence than in providing, " *throughout our colonies*, for the *decent* celebra-" tion of public religion". By which, accord-ing to his whole argument, he muft mean plant-ing *epifcopal* churches even in thofe colonies, where the people " have the means of religion " a'ready

" already, in *other proteſtant communions*". And who can doubt, but that this is a better way of *applying their munificence*, than ſending miſſionaries to the heathens, or only to the heatheniſh colonies, almoſt " abandoned to atheiſm and " infidelity !"

IN the laſt page, however, he talks in a rapturous ſtrain about " beholding this extenſive " country, juſt won to the Britiſh empire, *gra-* " *dually acceding*, AMONG *its numerous inhabi-* " *tants*, to the empire of JESUS CHRIST, and " of conſequence, flouriſhing in ARTS, in SCI- " ENCE", &c. The arts and ſciences are indeed very valuable in their places ; tho' they do not ſeem to be AMONG the primary or principal of thoſe important bleſſings, which flow from the knowledge and obedience of JESUS CHRIST. However, they are not to be deſpiſed. And who can doubt, but that they will be as much improved by the miſſion of ſo accompliſh'd a Scholar as Mr. *Apthorp*, in the confines of our *College*, as the religious ſtate of the country has been amended by the epiſcopal miſſions in general ? This was perhaps one deſign of the charitable Society therein ; that ſo the advancement of *learning* among us, may in time be as *greatly their work*, as the reformation of our religion is at preſent : I would hope, much more ſo—

AFTER quoting ſomething on this noble occaſion from VIRGIL, Mr. *Apthorp* concludes with ſome fine lines from Mr. POPE's MESSI-AH ; Tho' if he had either mentioned POPE's name, or mark'd them as a quotation, he might perhaps

perhaps at once have been thought lefs a *poet*
by the common people, and given ill-natur'd
critics lefs occafion to tax him as a *plagiary*.
Not that I myfelf in the leaft doubt his poetical
talents. For even in this *didactic* performance,
he has obliged us with many fpecimens of a fingular imagination, a florid, rhetorical diction, a
brifk, lively way of reafoning, marvellous turns
of argument, furprifing hyperboles, and divers
other *licences* even in grammar, truly poetical:
Nay, he has altered, not to fay *corrected* two of
thefe lines from Pope !

[Dum malè recitas, incipit effe *tuum* —]

Now, from a gentleman whofe profaic, argumentative compofitions are fo agreeably *be-
mufed*, what might not be expected, if he were to
write poetry *in earneft !*—But it may be doubted
whether he will be able to fpare time from his
more important concerns, to oblige the world in
this way ; efpecially if, as fome of late fuppofe,

——————————— " his reverend mind

" Begins to grow *right-rev'rendly* inclin'd"—

The CONCLUSION.

Whatever any may imagine, the author of the foregoing *Obfervations* ferioufly declares,that he heartily wifhes Mr. *Apthorp* well ; happy here and hereafter. And
if thefe obfervations fhould contribute any thing towards
fhewing him to himfelf, this will not tend to obftruct, but
to promote that benevolent end—

But the main end which he had in view, was much
more extenfive, general and important ;—that of ferving
the caufe of truth and righteoufnefs, of pure and undefiled religion in America : in diftinction from all private,
party-opinions whatfoever. He is very far from making
any

any pretensions to an exemption from mistakes. But as
to his sincerity, and the uprightnefs of his intentions; if
it were expedient to make proteftations in such cafes, he
could very cheartuliy appeal to that tribunal, at which
ALL are finally to appear.

NOTWITHSTANDING he is in principle and profeffion
an anti-epifcopalian; yet he fincerely loves and honors all
virtuous, candid and moderate men of all denominations
among Chriftians; by no means excepting thofe of the
epifcopal communion; with feveral of whom he has a
perfonal and agreeable acquaintance, which he would be
glad to keep up: Nor would he willingly and unnecef-
farily give offence to any perfons of that perfuafion.

Tho' he wifhes the people of New-England to ftand
faft in the liberty wherewith CHRIST hath made them
free; and not to return under that yoke of epifcopal
bondage, which fo miferably galled the necks of our
Forefathers, that they were not able to bear it, and therefore took refuge in America; yet he is far from
defiring to inflame the paffions of any one fect or party
againft another: So far from it, that he would fincerely
rejoice to be in the leaft degree inftrumental of uniting
them in the bonds of Chriftian charity, on the true plan
of the gofpel. In order to which, he cannot think an exact uniformity either in *fentiment*, or in modes of *worfhip* and *difcipline*, neceffary. The former is impoffible in this imperfect ftate, on divers accounts; and
the *latter* not to be expected, unlefs in countries where
the invaluable bleffing of liberty is facrificed to a far inferior object. Zealous attempts to eftablifh an exact
uniformity in religion, have generally, if not always
proved pernicious to the peace of fociety, to chriftian
charity and morals, in a very high degree: All ecclefi-
aftic hiftory is a proof of this. Such an uniformity, and
the advancement of the hierarchy, have too apparently
been favourite objects with the SOCIETY all along, particularly as to New-England; while the heathenifh colonies, the poor Negroes and Indians have been proportionably

onably neglected. And to what one valuable purpoſe?
—unleſs cauſing alienation of affections, and animoſities
among us, can be accounted ſuch!—And theſe are the
principal fruits which, conſidering the religious ſtate of
this country, can in reaſon be expected from a continued
proſecution of this deſign.

THE author concludes with his humble and earneſt
prayers, that GOD would unite all the SOCIETIES for the
propagation of TRUE RELIGION, whether in England,
Scotland or America, in a ſincere deſire to promote *that
alone ;* and afford them reſpectively ſuch lights and di-
rections as may ſerve to advance this one, ſingle, moſt
important end, to his own glory, and the good of mankind : till in the revolutions of times and ſeaſons, which
He keeps in his own power, " the GOSPEL OF THE
" KINGDOM ſhall be preached for a witneſs among ALL
" NATIONS"; and that grand event ſhall take place, in
praying for which all ſincere Chriſtians are already united ;—even that HIS KINGDOM may come, and HIS WILL
BE DONE ON EARTH AS IT IS IN HEAVEN. AMEN!

CORRECTIONS.

Page	line	from	read
16	8	top	or hurt
18	3	top	their charity
49	12	top	the name

N. B. 52. The firſt part of the marginal note there, ought to
have run thus, *viz.*
By what I can learn, there was no epiſcopal church in
N. England, 'till about An. 1685, or 1686, in the
reign of the infatuated roman-catholic K. *James* II,
and the adminiſtration of the roman-catholic Governor
Sir *E. Androſs.* Tho' K. *Charles* IId had before given
his allowance for one in Boſton, when our charter was
called into queſtion, An. 1679. It was at this time,
that, &c.

63	27	——	too often
69	12	top	is engaged.
87	1	bottom	too far
90	16	top	predeſtining
103	Title of Sect. 14,		to eſtabliſh
115	14	bottom	truth,

Religion in America
Series II

An Arno Press Collection

Adler, Felix. **Creed and Deed:** A Series of Discourses. New York, 1877.

Alexander, Archibald. **Evidences of the Authenticity, Inspiration, and Canonical Authority of the Holy Scriptures.** Philadelphia, 1836.

Allen, Joseph Henry. **Our Liberal Movement in Theology:** Chiefly as Shown in Recollections of the History of Unitarianism in New England. 3rd edition. Boston, 1892.

American Temperance Society. **Permanent Temperance Documents of the American Temperance Society.** Boston, 1835.

American Tract Society. **The American Tract Society Documents, 1824-1925.** New York, 1972.

Bacon, Leonard. **The Genesis of the New England Churches.** New York, 1874.

Bartlett, S[amuel] C. **Historical Sketches of the Missions of the American Board.** New York, 1972.

Beecher, Lyman. **Lyman Beecher and the Reform of Society:** Four Sermons, 1804-1828. New York, 1972.

[Bishop, Isabella Lucy Bird.] **The Aspects of Religion in the United States of America.** London, 1859.

Bowden, James. **The History of the Society of Friends in America.** London, 1850, 1854. Two volumes in one.

Briggs, Charles Augustus. **Inaugural Address and Defense,** 1891-1893. New York, 1972.

Colwell, Stephen. **The Position of Christianity in the United States,** in Its Relations with Our Political Institutions, and Specially with Reference to Religious Instruction in the Public Schools. Philadelphia, 1854.

Dalcho, Frederick. **An Historical Account of the Protestant Episcopal Church, in South-Carolina,** from the First Settlement of the Province, to the War of the Revolution. Charleston, 1820.

Elliott, Walter. **The Life of Father Hecker.** New York, 1891.

Gibbons, James Cardinal. **A Retrospect of Fifty Years.** Baltimore, 1916. Two volumes in one.

Hammond, L[ily] H[ardy]. **Race and the South:** Two Studies, 1914-1922. New York, 1972.

Hayden, A[mos] S. **Early History of the Disciples in the Western Reserve, Ohio;** With Biographical Sketches of the Principal Agents in their Religious Movement. Cincinnati, 1875.

Hinke, William J., editor. **Life and Letters of the Rev. John Philip Boehm:** Founder of the Reformed Church in Pennsylvania, 1683-1749. Philadelphia, 1916.

Hopkins, Samuel. **A Treatise on the Millennium.** Boston, 1793.

Kallen, Horace M. **Judaism at Bay:** Essays Toward the Adjustment of Judaism to Modernity. New York, 1932.

Kreider, Harry Julius. **Lutheranism in Colonial New York.** New York, 1942.

Loughborough, J. N. **The Great Second Advent Movement:** Its Rise and Progress. Washington, 1905.

M'Clure, David and Elijah Parish. **Memoirs of the Rev. Eleazar Wheelock, D.D.** Newburyport, 1811.

McKinney, Richard I. **Religion in Higher Education Among Negroes.** New Haven, 1945.

Mayhew, Jonathan. **Observations on the Charter and Conduct of the Society for the Propagation of the Gospel in Foreign Parts;** Designed to Shew Their Non-conformity to Each Other. Boston, 1763.

Mott, John R. **The Evangelization of the World in this Generation.** New York, 1900.

Payne, Bishop Daniel A. **Sermons and Addresses,** 1853-1891. New York, 1972.

Phillips, C[harles] H. **The History of the Colored Methodist Episcopal Church in America:** Comprising Its Organization, Subsequent Development, and Present Status. Jackson, Tenn., 1898.

Reverend Elhanan Winchester: Biography and Letters. New York, 1972.

Riggs, Stephen R. **Tah-Koo Wah-Kan; Or, the Gospel Among the Dakotas.** Boston, 1869.

Rogers, Elder John. **The Biography of Eld. Barton Warren Stone, Written by Himself:** With Additions and Reflections. Cincinnati, 1847.

Booth-Tucker, Frederick. **The Salvation Army in America:** Selected Reports, 1899-1903. New York, 1972.

Satolli, Francis Archbishop. **Loyalty to Church and State.** Baltimore, 1895.

Schaff, Philip. **Church and State in the United States** or the American Idea of Religious Liberty and its Practical Effects with Official Documents. New York and London, 1888. (Reprinted from *Papers of the American Historical Association,* Vol. II, No. 4.)

Smith, Horace Wemyss. **Life and Correspondence of the Rev. William Smith, D.D.** Philadelphia, 1879, 1880. Two volumes in one.

Spalding, M[artin] J. **Sketches of the Early Catholic Missions of Kentucky;** From Their Commencement in 1787 to the Jubilee of 1826-7. Louisville, 1844.

Steiner, Bernard C., editor. **Rev. Thomas Bray:** His Life and Selected Works Relating to Maryland. Baltimore, 1901. (Reprinted from *Maryland Historical Society Fund Publication,* No. 37.)

To Win the West: Missionary Viewpoints, 1814-1815. New York, 1972.

Wayland, Francis and H. L. Wayland. **A Memoir of the Life and Labors of Francis Wayland, D.D., LL.D.** New York, 1867. Two volumes in one.

Willard, Frances E. **Woman and Temperance:** Or, the Work and Workers of the Woman's Christian Temperance Union. Hartford, 1883.